Working Memories

Frome workers tell their stories

Home in Frome

Cover illustrations:
(front, from top left) Man in Black Swan yard; Evelyn Franks, née Smith, when a nurse; Winifred Fairhurst;
Beswick's workers; Singer's workers celebrate the firm's 150th anniversary

(rear) Frome Market Place in the 1940s (© Mary Evans Picture Library)

(endpapers) Extracts from a composite 1903 Ordnance Survey map of Frome, published by the Frome Society for
Local Study, hand-coloured by Rodney Goodall

Title-page illustration: a cast-iron lamp-post made by Cockey's in Frome

Contents-page illustration: Home in Frome's pop-up shop on Paul Street during the Frome Festival 2011

First published in 2012 by Home in Frome in association with Millstream Books

Set in Verdana, 11pt on 16.5, and printed in Great Britain by Butler Tanner & Dennis, Frome

© Home in Frome 2012

ISBN 978 0 948975 99 8

British Library Cataloguing-in-Publication Data:
a catalogue record for this book is available from the British Library

Contents

Introduction

Home in Frome is a community group celebrating, recording and sharing the unique character of Frome as it changes over time. It is in this spirit that we have produced *Working Memories*, a book of stories and images that reflect something of the complex working lives of people in Frome, beginning in the mid-1930s. We hope you enjoy it. We have deliberately restricted it to those events which are 'within living memory', since all the stories were collected in recorded interviews conducted between 2009 and 2012. These stories represent a tiny fraction of the total recorded material, which will now be deposited in the Somerset Archives. Some stories are sad, some happy, some simple, some complicated. We hope that all those who contributed to the book will feel that the stories we have chosen reflect well on them, and on the town where they have lived and worked. We hope that you, the reader, will enjoy these stories, and that they will stimulate your own interest in the town's history and pride in its heritage.

Inspiration came from Rodney Goodall's book, *The Industries of Frome*, published by Frome Society for Local Study. It was launched at the Robert Golden 'Home' exhibition at the Silk Mill in 2009, which set Home in Frome in motion.

Our approach is a rather different one, focusing on people's remembered experiences of working in some of Frome's occupations and industries, including factory work, production, health, education and the retail trade. Owing to demands on our time and the restricted space available in the book we have had to be selective regarding the number of occupations and businesses we have included. The oral histories collected also include memories of growing up and living in Frome. We want to try to convey to people today how people in the town lived, worked and played – and their feelings and thoughts. We have also highlighted the vital role played by Frome employers in making club facilities available for their employees' social life and in promoting Frome Carnival.

We have respected the wishes of those contributors who preferred to remain anonymous. Photographs of interviewees accompany their first words in the book. We have gone to some lengths to check names, dates, facts and spellings. Please let us know of any mistakes so that we can correct them in subsequent editions.

Contact us via the Home in Frome website (http://www.homeinfrome.org.uk/) or by writing to the Editor: John Payne, c/o Mortimer House, 9 Vallis Way, Frome BA11 3BD.

Acknowledgements

First of all our thanks to Jacqueline Peverley, whose energy and vision first led to the establishing of Home in Frome as a vibrant community group and who has contributed to this publication at every stage.

Thanks go to all members and supporters of Home in Frome for giving their support to the book's creation, conducting interviews, taking and copying photos, summarising and transcribing recordings, helping to put the text and photos together, and organising the publicity, workshops and book launch.

We would like to thank Tim Graham of Millstream Books of Bath who has overseen the typesetting and layout of the book, and Butler Tanner & Dennis of Frome for producing the book to a very tight schedule indeed and to the quality standards for which they are world famous.

Finally, to the people of Frome, past and present, who have responded magnificently to our requests for stories, information, photos and memories. Without you there would be no book. Thank you all.

Many local organisations have given us generous and invaluable support. They include Frome Carnival Committee, Frome Community College Media Arts department, Frome Museum, *Somerset Standard* and Somerset Archives. We would like to thank everyone who has kindly allowed us to use their photographs. Funding support has been received from The National Lottery through the Heritage Lottery Fund and from the Frome Society for Local Study.

Editor's Note

All the text set in ordinary type represents the words of the people who have recorded interviews for Home in Frome. The linking words in italics are my own. I hope they will help you to know not only who is speaking, but also the context of the stories and the links between them. If you do not notice them, they will have served their purpose. As always, my loving thanks to my wife Sandra, who continues to put up with a husband who refuses to retire.

John Payne
Home in Frome Editor
Frome, Somerset, 2012

We Didn't Know Any Different

HOME AND WORK IN FROME

SCHOOL

Daisy Bane, née Barry, born in 1919, was brought up in a large family in a substantial house in Broadway, and went to the Wesley School on Wesley Slope.

Daisy Bane

I had a happy childhood. Mum and Dad, they were very loving. I had a brother and four sisters, and we were a happy family, very happy. We always had plenty, we were lucky. Mother was always singing, she was

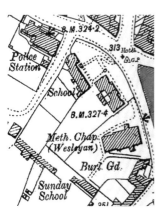

always happy, she was house-proud. The head-mistress was Miss Burchell and another teacher was Miss Ackland. My favourite teacher was Miss Dawes. She was the babies' teacher and she was Welsh. Miss Burgess, she was a lovely person, she was always smart. We always had our tunics and our nice white blouses and our blue ties, and our hats. I always remember how much they cost – two shillings and sixpence. That always stuck in my mind, 2/6 was a lot of money then.

We had four classes in the school and the boys' school was down the bottom next door to what used to be the police station [now the dance studio in Christchurch Street West]. And the police used to march and do drill in the boys' playground, and we used to watch. And we didn't have to make a noise, always remember that – mustn't make a noise, mustn't shout. **Daisy Bane**

Pupils and staff outside Wesley School, circa 1955

Val Humphries

Val Humphries had a rather different experience of childhood.

My mother died when I was seven, hence I went to the convent [St Louis Convent in Welshmill Lane, now St Louis School] as a boarder during the week. I used to come home at weekends but the reason I went there was because my father didn't want me being pushed from pillar to post. You know you could have come out of school and he could have said go to this neighbour, go to this friend, but he wanted it more stable for me. So I went there on a Monday morning and came home generally on a Friday evening or Saturday morning, and I was there to about 13, and then I went to Oakfield School. I can remember my aunt up in Fromefield, and she used to say, 'It used to break my heart Valerie to come up here and see you trying to iron shirts when you were eight or nine'.

Val Humphries

Staff and pupils at St Louis Convent, Welshmill Lane, about 1940

Cliff Ellis had a more formal education than many people in this book, culminating in a PhD.

Cliff Ellis

My mother put me into a private school, even though we were what you would call now working-class, no doubt about that, which was just down the road. The head was Miss Tucker, and there were about 15-20 of us from age four and what that meant was that when I went to my primary school, which was Christ Church on Park Road, I did extremely well. So then I moved from there to the Grammar School. I ended up getting an open scholarship to St Catherine's at Oxford and I got a degree in physics from Oxford, a First in fact, and then I stayed on and did research for nearly four years and hence I have a doctorate.

Below left, what remains of the Co-op bakery; below, marked in red, the route between Christ Church Primary School and Wesley School

Christ Church Primary School on Park Road, which is now residential, over the road there was a lane which went across to where Wesley School was. Half-way along there was the Co-op bakery. In the morning if we were clever, we could nip along there and buy some sticky buns. The bakery was where the Wesley pupils met the Christ Church pupils because we were very much against one another, there was quite a bit of antipathy. We played them at football on the odd occasion up on the Rec. **Cliff Ellis**

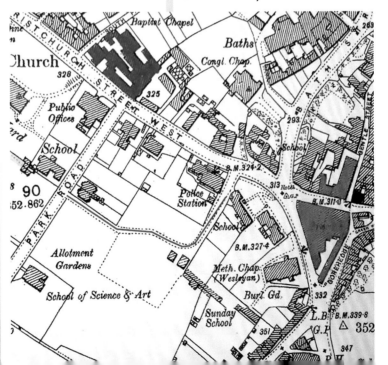

Right, Trinity School pupils taking part in a play pose for photos in the playground, late 1950s

Below, Bell Lane

Marion Barnes

Marion Barnes, née Sledge, was born in 1940 in Bell Lane, one of the streets in Trinity demolished in 1963. An only child, she attended Trinity School, now a private house, to the west of Trinity Church and Trinity Hall.

I started at Trinity School in 1944 when I was three-and-a-half. My father was one of 12 children, and they all attended Trinity School. So Miss Smith, who was then the infant school teacher, she knew the whole family and she agreed to take me at three-and-a-half because I used to cry after the children going to school. I felt left out! It was on the proviso that once I started it would be no good crying that I didn't want to come any more. I had to stay. So I did.

The only problem was that you had to go outside to go to the loo, and on a winter's day that could be quite cold! They looked after us quite well in the Infants. In the afternoon you had to have a nap, so you lay down on these little coconut mats, and tried to sleep for 20 minutes or half-an-hour. Yes, it was a good school, I enjoyed it at Trinity.

Marion Barnes

Milk Street School, now called Vallis First School, was often called the council school in contrast to the church schools. It was well equipped, and Daisy Bane remembers going down there once a week from the Wesley School to learn about laundry and cookery. Joan Smith's experience was not all good.

Joan Smith

I went to the council school down Milk Street. All my brothers and sisters went there too. I liked school but the honest truth was I was turned off because the teacher gave me the cane for something I didn't do. I don't know what I was supposed to have done. She just called me out and gave me the cane. I went home and my mum knew something was wrong. So my mum went down and had the teacher out and the headmaster and she said, 'I correct my children, so if you do it again, I'll do it to you'. So the next day I went back to school and they put me in another class and she had to apologise. I was about eight I suppose. I don't forget things like that.

Joan Smith

Isabel George, born 1920, also attended Milk Street School.

In those days the boys and the girls were completely separate. The girls were in the lower part of the area and the boys were upstairs. We had some super teachers, a lovely one called Miss Trowbridge – well, there were two Trowbridges, two sisters actually, and their father kept a

bakery in Buckland Dinham. One was tall and the other one was short, so they were known as Big Trow and Little Trow, and the senior mistress was a Miss Allwood, who was very fierce.

Isabel George

Isabel George

Left, a 1935 Silver Jubilee souvenir portrait taken for Frome Council School football team

11

Above, Milk Street School

Right, pupils from the late 1920s. Mavis Gray, who submitted the photo, stands at the back, second from left

Winifred Fairhurst

In the mixed classes in the senior school at Milk Street, things could sometimes get out of hand, but Mr Bell, the head, was able to combine humour and discipline, as Winifred Fairhurst, née Coleman, remembers.

I got into trouble, didn't I? As usual! You'll laugh about this one. A friend of mine was passing a letter to a boy and of course I had the letter in my hand and Mr Thorn – we used to call him Baggy Thorn – I don't know why, we had names for all the school teachers then. Anyway, I got caught with this letter. He wanted to know who I was passing it to and who it was from and I wouldn't tell him. Of course they were all laughing. In the end he said, 'We've caned one girl and now you're going to be the second one to be caned'. So I held my hand out and as he brought the cane down I took it away and everybody laughed. So I had to go to the headmaster. So of course Mr Bell and I were like this, we were great friends because I was friends with his daughter who was at the school then and I'd already been to tea the week before to his house, you see. 'Now what have you done Winifred?', he said. I told him and he laughed and I laughed and he said, 'Well, write out 100 times "I must not take my hand away when I am being caned"'. So I did those 100 lines and that was OK. Mr Thorn was a bit peeved about that because I did not get caned.

Winifred Fairhurst

The experience of the move from school to work was different for boys and girls. Girls either went straight into work or, like Isabel George, who studied art, went to do a course at the Park Road School of Art and Science, which in the post-war period was more like a small further education or technical college. Boys were more likely to get apprenticeships and attend college on day release.

Frome School of Art and Science

I wanted to do art, and I transferred to the Frome School of Art which was the college at the top of Park Road, opposite the hospital. I couldn't get all my training there – they didn't have life classes and one or two other subjects, so two days I went to Bristol, to the College of Art which in those days was at the top of Park Street, opposite the Victoria Rooms [in Bristol]. The train went through Radstock, Midsomer Norton, and the same people got on it, the half-past seven train from Frome station, the same people would get on it every morning and at some of the little stations like Hallatrow, the station-master would say, 'Don't go yet, just a minute, I'll see if she's coming'. It was a very enjoyable little ride for an hour.

Isabel George

The school occurs in this book with different names. It had a substantial community education programme which was transferred in 1989 to Frome College

HOUSING CONDITIONS

Gerald Quartley

Gerald Quartley, who was born in 1932, lived at Whitewell Road, which at that time was still surrounded by farmland.

It was very much a rural area. The Critchill Estate hadn't been built then, it was all farmland. Apart from mains water, we had no electricity or gas. There was a range, with an oven each side, the coal-house was under the stairs because the stairs went up circularly to the bedrooms, stone floors, but, you know, we didn't know any different really. My father drove a lorry for the council, Frome Rural District Council. All Mother did, she did some housework for people, some people in Keyford where she went to work when she left school, called Morgan, who were monumental masons. After I was born, she went back there to work.

Gerald Quartley

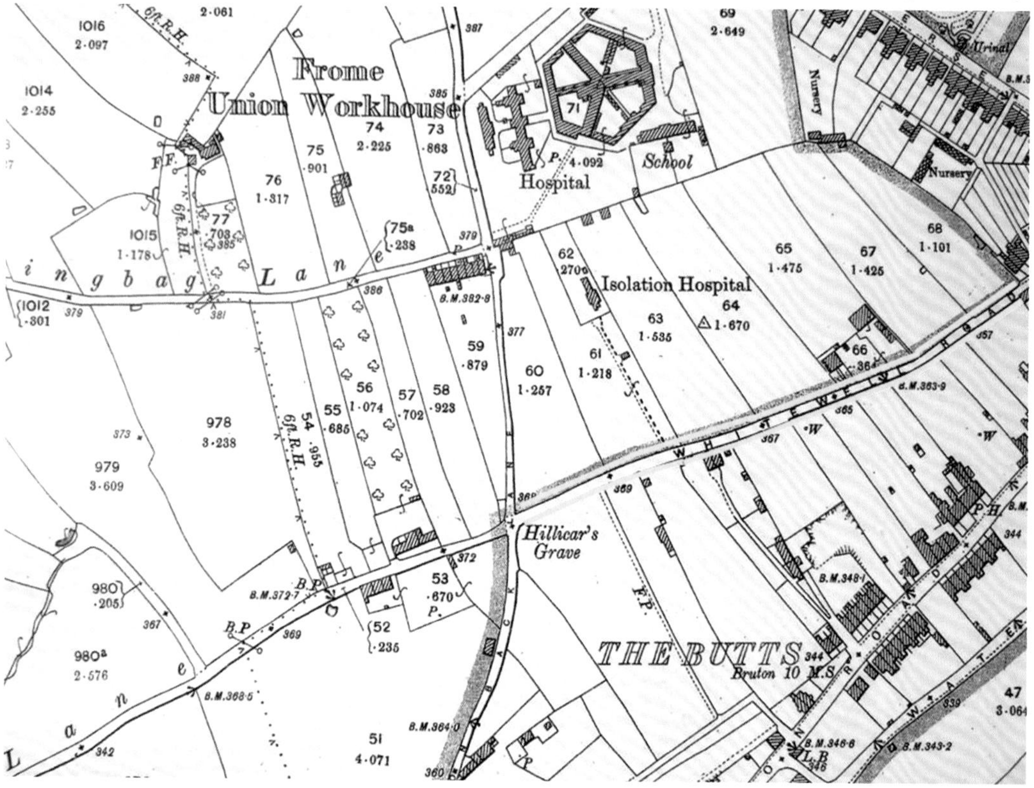

Whitewell Road, lined in yellow, as seen on a 1903 map, was not as built up as it is today

Dorothy Russell began her working life in service at a big house in Portway ('I had to do every chore she wanted done and she starved me') and then at Longleat House. On marriage, she went to live with her husband in Frome.

Dorothy Russell

He was from Frome, and he lived in a little cottage in Vicarage Street. You can just imagine living in Longleat House and then when I went to live in Vicarage Street I had no kitchen, no nothing, just a living room and bedroom. We had to share a toilet between three in the back yard. You had to put a stool down in the passage and wash yourself in a bowl of water. Number 20, and the house is still there now, I think. You had some steps and when you went up the steps it brought you out into Christchurch Street along the front, where Minty's shop was.

My first child was born at home at Vicarage Street. My husband had a job working on the railway and as soon as the midwife came, she said, 'You can get off to work, we don't want you hanging about! Yes', she said, 'You're getting in the way. Get off to work, she'll be all right'. **Dorothy Russell**

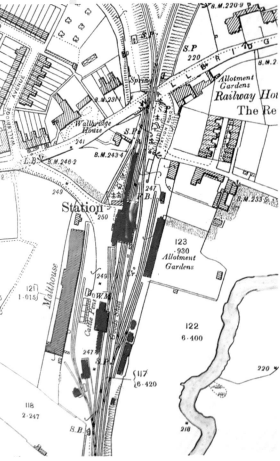

Left, an outside toilet in Trinity

Right, Dorothy's husband worked on the railway, seen here on a 1903 map, with the station buildings coloured red

15

Gwen Venn

Gwen Venn came to Frome when her husband got a teaching job here, and went to live in Willow Vale.

This cottage had no bathroom, no indoor toilet. You had to go across the back yard to get to what was really a garden shed, and the amusing thing about that was that instead of having a proper lavatory seat it had two planks going across for the lavatory seat. One had a big hole for the mother and the other had a little hole for the child, which just shows how old the cottage was. We had stone floors, and one open fire to heat the whole house.

My cottage was next to the railway line. Later on I was bathing both my sons in the bath, which was in the kitchen, and a train drew up outside. It was a tank engine and he knocked on the window and I opened it and he passed me a can and he said, 'Will you mash my tea for me?'. So I took the can in and put the kettle on, filled it up with boiling water. He waited and I passed it back, shut the window and that was that, although that wasn't so extraordinary in those days. No-one could believe that. I have measured my kitchen window and it is six feet two inches from the railway line. In fact my house holds up the railway line. You have to see it to believe it. I have lived here for 61 years, so I am the matriarch of Willow Vale. **Gwen Venn**

Below, Willow Vale; and below right, on one of the many occasions when it flooded

Sylvia Austin, née Wilson, born in 1943 at Milborne Port, and Tony Austin, born in 1937 at Upton Noble, moved briefly to Croydon, but came back to Frome in 1961.

On the corner of Church Lane there was a shop they did call Oily Morgan's. They used to deliver paraffin and other things all round the villages. And he had three cottages further down and we moved into the central one. It was a nice old cottage but one room down, one room up, toilet outside and a tap outside, but no electricity or running water

Sylvia and Tony Austin

inside. It was just gas lights and we had a gas boiler and a gas cooker. Right opposite there was a lovely old building, one that Frome Town Band used to practise in every Saturday morning. The next one up there was a lovely arch. And over the arch it said 'Soup Kitchen and Dispensary'. Eventually they pulled it down and the houses that we was living in was requisitioned because they was going to build a new class-room for St John's School right opposite.

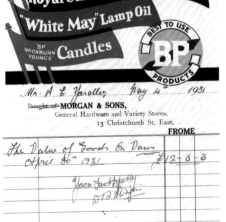

A 1931 invoice issued by Mr Morgan, and, far right, his shop in Christchurch Street East

GROWING UP IN FROME

One man who has lived most of his life in the Trinity area of Frome still remembers the noisy Sunday mornings.

I was born in Bath in 1941. The house that I was born in got bombed during the Bath Blitz. We came to live in Frome because my mother married a Frome chap. I was only a baby. The Trinity Boys' Band – I remember them because they used to march round Frome every Sunday. They used to make a hell of a row. It was a drum and bugle band, you see, and of course you'd get people lying in on Sunday morning, and they'd come round, bang, bang, bugles blowing. They used to march all round the streets, up Naish's Street, up through Horton Street, back down Broadway, and back down Selwood Road, back into the church.

Naish's Street, top; and left, members of Trinity Boys' Band perform in Trinity Street

Nowadays it's possible to grow up in Keyford or Trinity and be unaware of factories. Most of the firms that have survived are now out on the industrial estate. This was not the case for children growing up in the 1950s.

We lived in a little cottage in Keyford, opposite the Crown pub. There were five public houses when I was growing up in Keyford, now there's only one, the Crown. There was a builder's yard, Knight's. Over on the Butts was a huge builder's yard, Seward's. Behind where I lived was the cooperage. The brewery lorries would come there and bring the old barrels and they would come and collect the new wooden barrels and the huge wooden vats that they used in the brewing trade. And in the yard at the back they had all these huge planks ageing, maturing, all stacked, with separators in. So you looked in there and there were probably about three or four acres of wood which was being seasoned to become barrels.

Cliff Ellis

Workers at Wilson and Scotchman, a brewery engineering company at the cooperage, gather in front of stacks of oak planks that were seasoning to be used in making the brewery vats

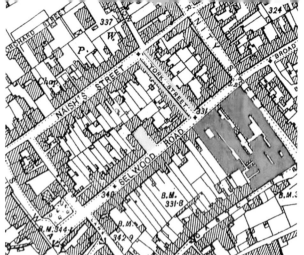

York Street and the 'Ope' outlined in yellow on a 1903 map

Winifred Fairhurst was born in 1921.

I was born at number 2, York Street, February the first, 1921. I was born at home and I was the youngest girl of eight children. There was four boys and four girls, and we lived in a three-bedroom house. The four girls were in one bed, two up the top and two down the bottom, and the boys were just the same in another bedroom. And Mum and Dad in another bedroom.

Winifred, aged 3

My childhood was absolutely wonderful! We weren't poor, but we were sort of medium. Food was very scarce but Dad had an allotment and he used to provide us all with the food. Mum used to take me and my sister, Phil, and my brother, down to market when I was about six or seven. My sister and I, we used to go down there and stand in front of the stall and I can remember I was very, very cheeky, saying, 'Oh, there is eight of us at home, you know, we need some cheap fruit and vegetables'. And I can remember the fruit man he used to say, 'Oh, there's that cheeky little 'b' again!'. He was very, very good, and my mum used to come home with loads and loads of stuff for about two shillings. **Winifred Fairhurst**

The 'Ope' in Selwood Road before the Trinity redevelopment

Alan is Winifred's son and a Trinity boy through and through. The family lived in the 'Ope', the little setback of houses in Selwood Road which the local children called the 'Hope'.

I was born in the Hope in Selwood Road. It's a little square half way down Selwood Road. Originally there were, I think, three cottages on the left-hand side and I think there are now two.

They were put into one and I lived in the middle one with my mum and my dad who was in the army at the time. We had one room downstairs, one room upstairs and me and my brother and my mum lived there. We had a little scullery which was just a cooker and a sink. Outside tap, cold water shared between two cottages. Down the bottom of the garden on the right we had the toilets and the boiler where we used to do all the cleaning of clothes. It was about a 20 yards walk. **Alan Fairhurst**

Alan Fairhurst

Peter Street

Left, a young Trinity resident stands in front of Nos. 1 and 2 Peter Street, outlined in yellow on a 1903 map

One man remembers growing up in Trinity in one of the streets that was demolished in 1968.

I was born in number 1, 2 and 3, Peter Street. My granddad had number 1, my dad had number 2, and bought number 3, knocked it into one big house. All the poor people used to live in this part of the town. People actually couldn't go any further down, you went up the ladder from here. So everyone who came into Chinatown wanted to better themselves.

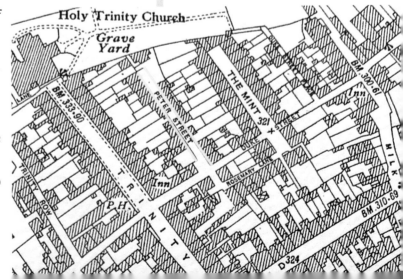

Ron White

Ron White grew up in Waterloo, just across what is now the Jenson Button Bridge from the Market Yard.

Well, when I was a boy, there was a lovely iron bridge and there was this rank, I think it was about 12 or 14 in a hammerhead, of three-storey Victorian houses. I suppose previous to us living there it must have been all the mill workers' houses. And at the bottom of the road just before you got to the bridge, on the corner of the river there, was the remains of a mill, when I was a boy. It still had walls and windows, which we used to play in. But that's totally disappeared now.

Inside the house, conditions were much like those in many other older Frome houses in the 1930s and 1940s.

In the living room we had one gas-lamp and a black range. Then you had a scullery, no kitchens in those days, with a boiler in the corner of the scullery that you lit to get the hot water. There was a big Norfolk sink and one cold water tap, and that was it, apart from the boiler which you lit every Monday to do the washing. At the back you had just a square yard with a toilet and coal-house, no garden at the back at all. You had a big tin bath hung on a hook in the yard, and you took the bath in, put it in front of the range, and you lit the boiler, got the hot water going, then took it into the living room and put it in the bath and had a bath. Once a week, Saturday night. **Ron White**

The area of Frome called Waterloo, across the river from the Market Yard, shown here on a 1903 map

Like Alan Fairhurst, Trevor Weston was brought up in the 'Ope', though he is also sure the local children referred to this as the 'Hope'. Like many Frome people of his generation, he remembers Trinity as 'Chinatown'.

I worked for pocket money, you know. I didn't have to work. Molly, she used to work on the dairy [Mount Pleasant Dairy], and I used to go round with her Saturdays and Sundays delivering the milk. And then when I got a bit older, I had two paper rounds in the mornings, and I used to work for Mr Rossiter's in the evenings delivering the groceries.

As I was told, before the war you called it, Trinity which was the church, and the Americans come during the war, I was told, which is obviously right, that every big city in America had what they called a Chinatown ghetto, and the Yanks called it that – 'We'll see you down Chinatown' – and it just lived on. It's a generation thing. People what grew up with me, we always still call it Chinatown. **Trevor Weston**

Below left, Trinity Row

Below, Britannia Stores, which was run by Mr Rossiter, on the corner of Naish's Street

23

Bob Norris

Below, Bob Norris and his brother Dan at work on Sandy's Hill Farm, 1985

For children of farming families, helping on the farm was part and parcel of growing up.

Bob Norris came to Sandy's Hill Farm on the western fringe of Frome at the age of five in 1950, when his father bought the farm, and has been there ever since. He attended Oakfield Road School and reflects on differences between town and country children.

We were expected to work more, we had our jobs to do on the farm. When you came back home you helped out with the milking or helped turn cows around or feed calves or something like that. Most days you'd have the same routine jobs.

And on leaving school he went to work on the farm.

I don't like working indoors, not really, especially if you get a nice day. I had day release and went to Norton-Radstock College one day a week to learn about agriculture – growing crops and livestock – and a fair bit with machinery, because machinery was getting more of an in-thing. People had gone from horses to machines. There was quite a bit on welding and that sort of thing. My father, he worked with horses, my brother-in-law, he worked with horses. I think people were happier with horses. You can talk to a horse, you can't talk to a machine, can you?

My father didn't retire, he died when he was about 70. Now there's me and my brother, partners, and then I've got my son working. My wife, she helps as well, a few hours a day. My son was quite keen to do it. He could have got on at school if he'd wanted to, he was good enough to take his 'A' levels and go on to university. I've got another son that went to university. When I left school Father had about 16 or 20 cows. I expect we've got 180 now, you see.

Bob Norris

Gloria Wingrove, born in 1950, moved to Lullington, just outside Frome, in the same year. Her father worked as a dairy farmer.

Gloria Wingrove

It was the best childhood I could ever have had, and so many children will never have that. We lived in a thatched cottage. My favourite memories are every spring my dad would bring home a little lamb, at least one, sometimes two or three, that had been abandoned by the mother, and we had to feed them up until they were fit enough to go back to the farm, which used to break our hearts! But as we got a little bit older we used to go up to the farm with our dad and we used to feed all the calves, with great big bottles of milk.

I was one of seven children but there was two other families that had children the same ages, or similar ages, to us, and we all used to play together. One farmer, he used to grow potatoes and we used to help pick them up when they were ploughing them up, and to get us into the field, we all had to sit on the back of a trailer and we'd bounce all along the lanes and across the fields. Mum used to send us out to collect wood for the fires, so that was our winter job. We had a huge allotment, they'd probably put about 20 houses on it today, but we all had our own little plots and we had to grow veg to help Father with the workload.

Gloria Wingrove

A cattle birth notification card from 1935

Daisy aged 17

Inset right, a programme from a Butler and Tanner's employees' outing to London in 1929

Diana Ingram

MARRIED LIFE

For many women, work ended with marriage, a decision often imposed on them by husbands or fathers, as Daisy Bane remembers.

I went to Houston's when I was 14 and I got married [in 1938] when I was 20. I never worked after. Father and my mother didn't believe in us going to work after getting married. He made us save, he made us save a little bit every week – oh yes, Father was like that! – so we should have some money when we got married. **Daisy Bane**

Diana Ingram, née Lewis, did a secretarial course at Frome Art and Science College in Park Road [now the site of a block of retirement flats] and was secretary to Captain Fleming, the managing director of Butler and Tanner.

I think it was my parents' choice but in those days I have to say there were lots of jobs available. That was it, and obviously my parents thought I should go to Butler and Tanner's, so I went. When I got married, I stopped working, I had to. My husband said I had to stop working. Not very happy at the time, but I bowed to the convention, because everybody did. I mean, there was no need for me to stop work at all.

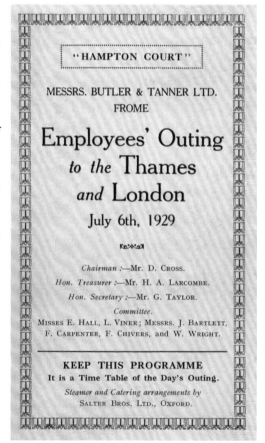

"HAMPTON COURT"

MESSRS. BUTLER & TANNER LTD.
FROME

Employees' Outing *to the* Thames *and* London

July 6th, 1929

Chairman :—Mr. D. Cross.
Hon. Treasurer :—Mr. H. A. Larcombe.
Hon. Secretary :—Mr. G. Taylor.
Committee.
Misses E. Hall, L. Viner; Messrs. J. Bartlett,
F. Carpenter, F. Chivers, and W. Wright.

KEEP THIS PROGRAMME
It is a Time Table of the Day's Outing.

Steamer and Catering arrangements by
Salter Bros. Ltd., Oxford.

I didn't have any children until I'd been married for three years. In those days I was conventional, I won't say I am now, I've grown out of it!

Diana Ingram

Margaret Whorlow was another woman for whom working life ended with the birth of her children.

I did work during the war but that was before I was married. I carried on working for a little while until Paul came along and Anthony came after that. I used to go out as much as I possibly could. I belonged to the church, Christ Church, and I still have a lot to do with that now. Then I used to belong to the Mothers' Union. I've belonged to that for years, ever since I was married. They used to meet once a week, now it's a monthly meeting combined with St John's and Trinity. When we were younger with our children, the older members used to say, 'Oh dear! Not children again!'. And they didn't like it. They would have a speaker that used to come and talk about different things and what they had done in life and that sort of thing and when we didn't have a speaker, we would kind of amuse ourselves, knitting and things like that.

Margaret Whorlow

Margaret Whorlow

Frome Mothers' Club 1983 Frome Carnival entry HMS Fish Finger

Dorothy Hawker

Dorothy Hawker's husband was a carpenter, and building trades were always the first to suffer in a recession, as they are today.

We had a couple of lean times, didn't we? But you didn't seem to want so much, d'you know what I mean? As long as you had your everyday running things you managed all right. I mean, we didn't have a car, but that didn't matter, we were quite happy, we used to do a lot of walking, push the kids about in buggies, go down the fields and they used to paddle, take a picnic and things like that. And then of course Crown Tours [at The Butts] was running, which we didn't live far from. We used to book up and go to the seaside for a day out, usually Weymouth or Weston. Or the zoo!

Dorothy Hawker

Vallis Vale, above, was a popular place for family picnics and Crown Tours offered a variety of excursions, as in this 1937 advert

CROWN GARAGE TOURS

'Phone 146.

SSUNDAY, September 23rd—

9 a.m.	BOURNEMOUTH *via* NEW FOREST	...	Return 6.30 p.m.	FARE	6/6
2 p.m.	WESTON-S-MARE *via* CHEDDAR	...	Return 8 p.m.	FARE	5/–
6 p.m.	SHEARWATER	...	...	FARE	1/6

TUESDAY, September 25th—

9 a.m.	WEYMOUTH ...	...	Return 6.30 p.m.	FARE	6/–
2 p.m.	STOURTON ...	...	...	FARE	2/–

THURSDAY, September 27th—

9 a.m.	BOURNEMOUTH *via* NEW FOREST	...	Return 6.30 p.m.	FARE	6/6
2 p.m.	WESTON-SUPER-MARE *via* CHEDDAR	...	Return 8 p.m.	FARE	5/–
5 p.m.	WOOKEY HOLE CAVES	...	...	FARE	2/9

SUNDAY, September 30th—

8 a.m.	PORTSMOUTH AND SOUTHSEA	...	Return 6.30 p.m.	FARE	7/6
9 a.m.	WEYMOUTH ...	...	Return 6.30 p.m.	FARE	6/–
2 p.m.	WESTON-SUPER-MARE *via* CHEDDAR	...	Return 8 p.m.	FARE	5/–
6 p.m.	SHEARWATER	...	...	FARE	1/6

THE BUTTS, FROME.

BOOK EARLY TO AVOID DISAPPOINTMENT.

TOWN BOOKING OFFICE—Mr. SHARLAND, Cheap Street.

You Could Buy Anything in Frome

A SHOP ON EVERY CORNER

People in Frome will tell you that once upon a time you could shop all the way from Badcox to the Market Place. And it's true! While Catherine Hill is still lined by shops, in Catherine Street many of them have been converted back into homes. Janet Ruddick remembers the shops that were there.

Janet Ruddick

Catherine Hill

Reproduced by permission of English Heritage

Catherine Street has changed beyond all imagination. It was full of shops. Coming from Badcox into Catherine Street itself there was Oatley's the grocer, then the butcher's which is now Cayford's, Difazio's motor-cycle shop and a greengrocer/general stores on the corner of Catherine Street and Morgan's Lane. Continuing down that left-hand side were Mr Biancoli the tailor, Mrs Markey's second-hand and antique shop, Watt's the cycle-shop, Ayres' the greengrocer and Case the meat shop. Selwood Dairy, run by the Bastins, came next, then the entrance to the Piggeries, a scruffy cut through to Castle Street. The farther side of the opening was

Difazio poster 1954

Frank Pellow's shop

Kathleen Applegate's the dress shop. Beyond came a little grocer's followed by Williams' the butcher and Pellow's the ironmonger. Knight and Morris [furniture] came next followed by Knight's, a long block, later called Lees', which sold fabrics, ladies clothes, and a curtain-making service. Then Sutton's, electrical goods, Hobbs' the butcher's and Mr Genge the gentlemen's outfitters. You are now at the top of Whittox Lane.

On the right-hand side there were no shops before the Sun Inn. Beyond Badcox Lane Baptist Church [now flats called Catherine Court] there was Tuff's the greengrocer and florist's later run by the daughter and son-in-law, Mr and Mrs Roberts. Then came Bell's, the photographer and camera shop, followed by Taylor's cycle shop. The Temperance Hall [later used as Frome library], which stood between the last two, had to be demolished when it became unsafe. Then came Williams' cooked meat shop where Miss Starr would serve you.   **Janet Ruddick**

Catherine Street shops

In Trinity, before the slum clearance and redevelopment of the 1960s, 1970s and 1980s, there were a lot of shops too.

Mr Olding at 51, Trinity Street. That's all long gone. That all went in the Trinity clearance. [He sold] brushes, brooms, mops, doormats, kitchen utensils. I remember on the corner they used to cook their pigs' feet, one of the delicacies of Frome – faggots and pigs' feet. They used to cook their own on the corner, opposite the Lamb and Fountain. It's all gone now in the clearances.

As Trevor Weston recollects:

And everybody went to the little shops, there were no supermarkets. A shop on every corner. Mr Dickens on the corner of York Street and Selwood Road. Then you went further down still, where the King's Head was, you had a Co-op store on the corner.

Round the corner in Trinity Street you could find

Mr Upshall's greengrocer's, then further along you had a butcher's, then you had Holborn's fish-and-chip shop, everybody said that was the best fish-and-chips ever. If you went the other way, back towards the Piggeries, you had a hardware shop, an ironmonger's you'd call it today. You could get anything you wanted in there: paraffin, hammers, nails, screws, there was no need to go out the area at all really.

Trevor Weston

Upshall's Groceries 2012

Upshall's has survived in Selwood Road, just round the corner from Trinity Street near the new flats, and is now run by Mike Upshall, grandson of the shop's first owner, Jessie Upshall.

Trinity Clearances 1969

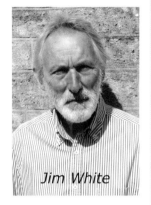

Jim White

THE IDEAL WATCH FOR
ROUGH WEAR
+
GUARANTEED UNBREAKABLE
& WATERTIGHT !
+
THE "VERTEX" REVUE SPORT WRISTLET

FITTED WITH
SHOCK-
ABSORBING
SPRINGS,
ENCASED.
NON-
MAGNETIC
PRECISION
LEVER
MOVEMENT

PRICES:
Gent.'s Model - £3 : 0 : 0
Ladies' Model - £3 : 12 : 0

WRITE OR ASK FOR ILLUSTRATED LEAFLET.
+
HERBERT J. WHITE (LATE GEORGE THICK)
THE BRIDGE, FROME. (Tel. 135.)

Below left and centre: Herbert and Jim White's jewellery and clock shop on The Bridge

KEEPING SHOP

As a boy, Jim White started work in his father's jewellery, watch and clock shop on The Bridge in 1957. He finally sold the business in 1987 and retrained as a stonemason.

Everything came to life on Wednesdays because it was market day and we were right next to the market. But even in the 1950s, retail trade was going away from The Bridge, moving more to the centre of the town. So in the end, in 1971, I closed the shop and moved up to Cheap Street. It was mostly jewellery and watches, and a huge amount of repair work, which I was involved in. We used to work right up in the attic from where you could look down the river. It was quite lethal really! We used to wash clocks in petrol, something that nowadays would never be allowed because the whole lot could have gone up in smoke at any time. Needless to say the older watchmakers at work used to smoke all the time as well.

The most important thing was that 90% of the shops were owned by local people. So all the money spent in the town stayed in the town and it circulated in the town all the time. There were only a couple of multiples, one of which was the International Stores. There were hardly any empty [shops]. Cheap Street was always busy, always full, and Catherine Hill was shops top to bottom. There were lots and lots of food shops and the whole town was self-contained. My own grandmother ran a little tiny shop until the mid 1950s in Wine Street. So the family has always been involved in retailing, and her family was involved in the baking business which was in Catherine Hill. ***Jim White***

Ken Miller inherited a family ironmonger's in Keyford, but had to move several times to keep his business afloat. He also travelled round the villages selling paraffin as well as ironmongery.

Ken Miller

Although we were mainly ironmongers, we had hardware and china and glass in the Keyford shop. So we had quite a range of goods from barbed wire for the farmers down to china tea sets, you see, all sorts of things like that. You used to have a big tank inside the vehicle, then we had the glass sides where we used to put all the hardware and china and glass. Because in those days there was no electricity in the villages, and they used to cook with paraffin and light with paraffin. They just had ordinary paraffin lamps, you see.

By 1954 they had moved into a town centre shop, in Bath Street, which was a busy shopping street.

We decided to buy another ironmonger's in Catherine Street. And the reason we bought that was because they had a Calor gas agency and they were the only agency in the town, for gas, and of course we bought that and of course that did us quite good because when electricity came to the villages and the paraffin died out we had another product there to sell. Then my father took over that business and I carried on in Bath Street.

Mr and Mrs Miller, above, and shop below

33

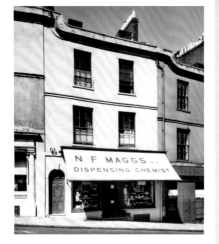

Shops in Bath Street

Both pictures reproduced by permission of English Heritage

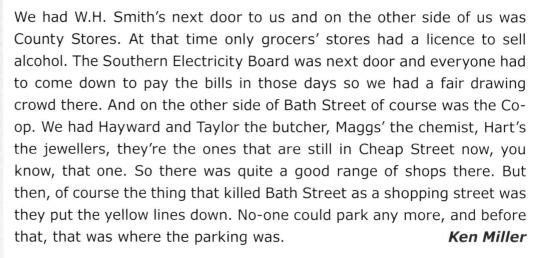

We had W.H. Smith's next door to us and on the other side of us was County Stores. At that time only grocers' stores had a licence to sell alcohol. The Southern Electricity Board was next door and everyone had to come down to pay the bills in those days so we had a fair drawing crowd there. And on the other side of Bath Street of course was the Co-op. We had Hayward and Taylor the butcher, Maggs' the chemist, Hart's the jewellers, they're the ones that are still in Cheap Street now, you know, that one. So there was quite a good range of shops there. But then, of course the thing that killed Bath Street as a shopping street was they put the yellow lines down. No-one could park any more, and before that, that was where the parking was.

Ken Miller

Diane Rouse, born in 1935, came to Frome as an evacuee – and stayed!

My earliest memory of shopping in Frome, well I was an evacuee in the War and stayed here. I came down here with my grandma and of course I used to go shopping with her, but very, very different in those days. Things were so hard to get, this is in the Forties, grandma used to buy second-hand clothes, take them home, unpick them, wash them and make them up on the wrong side for me, but even in the Fifties shopping was quite bustling in Frome then. I'd go to shopping with my dad and it would just be a trip into Wickenden's in the Market Place, that was the cake shop, and we always bought a fresh cream sponge every Saturday and took it home and ate it for our tea.

Shopping in the Market Place in the 1930s

Diane ran a fashion shop on Catherine Hill from 1974-1994.

I was in partnership with my mother, and we had a shop at 21 Catherine Hill. I well remember the first day when we opened. Playing on the radio was the hit tune of that year, Maria Muldaur's 'Midnight at the Oasis', and as we opened the door the first customer came in – much to my surprise! And I can remember what we sold her too – a pale blue broderie anglaise blouse. And that was the start of 21 happy years on Catherine Hill.

Fashions of that day, it was hot pants, which were very short, micro or mini shorts – a lot of them had a bib-and-brace top, tank tops were popular, and then came the bell bottom trousers, very, very flared and of course very big platform shoes.

The fashion shops on the Hill would put on a show together. And there was Maidment's Fabrics on the High Pavement, she would join in as well. They made bridal wear which was really nice. And there was a hairdresser's on the Hill called Lunatic Fringe. And altogether it was really a happy, bustling place.

Diane Rouse

Diane Rouse

The window of Diane's shop on Catherine Hill

Dennis Barnard is another shopkeeper who went into the family business.

It was always recognised that eldest sons of family grocers would go into the business. Having left school I joined the family business in Chapmanslade. I left school one day and started work the next day for two years. Then I did National Service for two years. I finished National Service on the Thursday morning and I started back at work in the shop on Thursday afternoon. Not too many holidays in those days.

That is why I particularly enjoyed National Service which was a very important part of my life because I went from being part of a village shop, talking about babies arriving, illness, whether the washing was dry, and going into a man's world. I am quite sure I was more mature at 18 at that stage than any child is now.

Dennis Barnard

Dennis Barnard

Tony Paniccia

Below, the Paniccia family enjoy their own ice-cream

In Frome, and in many surrounding towns and villages from the Mendips to Salisbury, ice-cream meant Paniccia's.

We had an ice-cream business, family concern, my grandfather and father started it up in 1926, that's before I was born. I was born in Frome in 1932 and I'm one of eight, and number seven in the whole lot! We used to make ice-cream, deliver round the villages and towns as far as 30 miles apart. My eldest brother, Albert, used to get up in the morning and make the mix and I or my brother, John, would be at the factory at quarter to five with the machines running, freezing the ice-cream ready to take out in the vans to sell. We used to get up, do the factory work, come home, have a wash and shave and change, have a quick bit of breakfast or dinner and then go out and return home about half-past eight at night. The whole factory finished at Christmas 1991, when my cousin from Yeovil with the same name of Paniccia bought the business as a running concern.

Initially, Tony's father sold fruit on market stalls with ice-cream on the side, but ice-cream became the more important side of the business. When ice-cream production finally finished, the factory building in Naish's Street was replaced by two bungalows, the garage [originally a non-conformist chapel] was converted into flats, called Paniccia Court, and the shop reverted to a house.

Until I retired in 1991 I didn't have a summer holiday, none of us did. If anything had to be done, it had to be done in January or February. So I got married on January the 20th 1962.

When we started we had one van, then in 1939 my father bought these two vehicles, they were before their time, two Rio Silver Crowns. If you wanted to hear their engine run, you had to rev it up, they were so quiet. And the little boy on the doors, don't matter what position you were, he was looking at you. And on the roofs inside you had the clouds and bluebirds on the ceiling. They were marvellous. And there was a long mirror as well so people used to look and adjust their ties and their hair and everything. They used to be painted by Hodder's of Frome afterwards, to keep them up to scratch because children with their coins used to scrape or tap on the vehicle and chip all the paint, but they were made in Bristol.

Tony Paniccia

Pauline Rodgers is Tony Paniccia's sister and was born in Frome in 1930. Their grandparents had come from the south of Italy to settle in the town.

I used to go out on the vans with my sister, Vera. We used to go to Radstock on a Monday and Frome market, and the others used to go to Salisbury market, then Chippenham on a Friday, all round. I used to go with Vera to Bath on a Sunday, and on a Thursday I used to go with our dad. I was 14, just left school, and I worked for them until I got married when I was 19. It was all family. Later, when we all got married and left, they did have workers, including Bill Webber and Bill Uphill. One was big and the other small, they used to call them Big Bill and Little Bill.

At the factory

Like their many customers, Pauline remembers the shop in Naish's Street.

There was two tables, and four chairs, that's all. People used to sit there waiting, and some used to have ice-cream sundaes. It was in a tall glass, and you'd put fruit at the bottom, then the ice-cream, the strawberry and the vanilla. At Christmas Albert did use to do a chocolate one as well, though he didn't like to do it.

Pauline Rodgers

Pauline Rodgers

Dowling's was another gents' outfitters on Catherine Hill

BEHIND THE COUNTER

One interviewee worked for a men's outfitters, Bradley's in Catherine Hill, and recalls some keen competition.

We were in competition with Hodge's which was just down Stony Street. We had advertising in the shop window saying we were more reasonable. I remember one time when Bradley's did an advert in the cinema and we had free tickets to go and see what the advert was like. We used to sell school uniforms for all the schools round Frome: Oakfield Road, Christ Church, Trinity, all schools round Frome, except for the Grammar School, but Hodge's used to stock the [boys] Grammar School uniforms [Fosters stocked the uniform for girls]. You had to have a school cap, a scarf, blazer, badge, grey flannel trousers, grey flannel shorts, socks, that was the school uniform then, you see.

I worked from nine, and we used to have an hour for dinner, then till six at night. Thursday was half-day closing. I didn't get on too well with the shop work. I was there four or five years and every morning my job was to clean those windows, every morning without fail! I had to clean all around the woodwork, round the window. And I used to have a chamois leather and a little pair of steps and a bucket of water.

There were a lot of funny things. For a start, there was the manager, and there was the assistant manager, and they were in competition with one another, because they got commission on what they sold. And very often there were arguments over what customers they'd served, because one wanted a suit and one only wanted a tie, and they wanted the one with the most commission.

Margaret Whorlow worked at Frome Co-op in the 1930s and then through the Second World War. She was in a food department, which was a reserved occupation.

I left school at 14 and I went as a shop assistant in the Co-op in Bath Street. The Co-op started right from round the corner from Stony Street and it went all along Palmer Street and down and round into Bath Street. It started at the butcher's and then it went to the grocer's, it went to the shoe shop and then it went to the chemist, then it went round to Bath Street.

There was a ladies' clothes shop on the corner, then it was a men's clothes shop, then it was the cake shop and the café upstairs. That was all the Co-op. I worked in the cake shop. There was a café upstairs, so as well as serving downstairs in the shop, bread and cakes and things like that, you also had to help if you saw people going up the stairs for a cup of coffee or a meal. You had to go and see what they wanted. It was up and downstairs, up and downstairs! During the War, I worked there all the time, because I didn't have to go into the army or navy or air force. It was food you see.

Margaret Whorlow

Co-op advertisement 1951

Co-op stores at the corner of Palmer Street and Bath Street

Above, Co-op token

Left, Co-op advertisement

Going to the auction

Auctioneers at Frome Fatstock Market 1990

Geoff Sheppard and Clive Vincent

OFF TO MARKET

Frome has always been the market town for the farming community of north-east Somerset, as Geoff Sheppard and Clive Vincent make clear.

Frome's our local market town. My father and all his generation, market day was their day. They always went on a Wednesday. My father would always dress up, collar and tie, to go to market, and he would never miss unless he was ill. It didn't matter what you had on, he would always go to market. And I think probably it was their day out and they socialised with the rest of the farming community. I can remember the Flora Café in Cheap Street [now the Settle], and on a Wednesday people'd be queuing up, they'd queue to wait and sit down because everyone went there for their lunch. **Geoff Sheppard**

Market day was a huge thing for everyone. The market pulled people together. You went there with your calves or your sheep or your pigs or cows, whatever it might be, whether you were buying or selling, but it was also just a wonderful place to meet your friends and neighbours, because you'd know most people there. And when the market was down in the old Market Yard, it'd be chock-a-block on a Wednesday, you couldn't move, the place was just solid with traffic. **Clive Vincent**

The moving of the market out of town and the building of two out-of-town supermarkets has made Frome a quieter, but much less lively place. A lot of buying and selling went on in the Market Hall and the yard of the Black Swan. Auctioneer Dennis Barnard has vivid memories of the market.

The Black Swan public house, where the Black Swan galleries are now, that was a derelict pub. The yard that is now quite posh with chairs and tables, that was the yard in which we sold geese and chickens and rabbits and pigeons and ferrets and budgerigars and all sorts of livestock. At the back of the Black Swan yard there was the offices for the cattle market which was on the other side, where the Cheese and Grain is now. There was such congestion there all the time, with the stalls, with the lorries coming in and out, very lively, very noisy. There would be a huge variety of things on sale – basic things like eggs and poultry, fruit and vegetables, cream, people wouldn't dream of buying them from the shop, they would buy them from the market. Those things that are needed to be fresh would be bought from the market, canned goods and other things would be bought from the local shop.

Congestion in Market Yard

Unloading livestock

I well remember Edgar and Emily Parfitt, brother and sister who lived in Chapmanslade, and who grew vegetables in a very old-fashioned way, all the work being done by hand. They would go to Frome with the horse and a flat cart and would park up just off Justice Lane in the Market Place, and set up their stall, and would sell their vegetables. There were two other men, Walt and Ted Leonard, great characters, just had a cart. They would grow vegetables and on Wednesdays and on Saturdays, they would push this cart round the back streets of Frome, and sell the vegetables, and then buy lots of drink on the way home. Their needs were very few and they enjoyed life! **Dennis Barnard**

The Round Tower in 1989

Auctioneers at work

In the Black Swan yard

Cattle could be loaded and unloaded direct from the Frome-Radstock railway using the ramp which can still be seen next to the Cheese and Grain Hall. Ron White was brought up in Waterloo, just across the river. Ron also explains why Justice Lane is so called.

The market yard used to be our playground when we were kids, having lived just over the river. When I was a kid the Round Tower was all fallen down with no roof on it, but just round the corner from that was a family called Prince. And I was friendly with them. So there was a group of kids round here, that came from Willow Vale and round this area, we always used to play here in the market.

I can remember hundreds and thousands of cattle coming down that ramp, you'd have a job to imagine it now, but the trains would come in with the cattle trucks, and hundreds and hundreds of Irish cattle would come down that ramp. And the Irish drovers used to come over with them. There was a platform up the top, and they had the cattle trucks with the doors on the side, and they'd open the doors and drive the cattle out and straight down here. My father got to know one of the old Irish drovers very well, and he used to stay with us at Waterloo. They were here for weeks but they used to have to drive these cattle way out into the country to store them before they could bring them in and sell them.

Where you come down Justice Lane, opposite the Black Swan, where the car-park is now, there was a big house there and of course that used to be the old Frome Police Station. That's why it's called Justice Lane. Then they moved the police station up to the top of Bath Street, in Christchurch Street West. And when you got done here for anything, they said, 'Oh, you know, he's had to go up the steps', because if you notice outside of that building are loads and loads of steps. They never used to say, 'He's got prosecuted', they'd say, 'He's going up the steps next week'.

Ron White

As a girl, Liz Symes made money from selling stock at Frome market.

Dennis Barnard and David Millard were very good auctioneers, they could sell anything to everyone. In the Black Swan yard on Wednesday there were chickens, rabbits and smaller stock in cages. At the time when I was 10 or 11, I remember we had rabbits at home, it was Easter, Dad purchased three does and one buck. Each time I cleaned them out I'd stick them in together, so at one point we had 40 New Zealand Whites which we then took to the market and I believe I had half-a-crown per head of rabbit!

Liz Symes

Liz Symes

Quintyn Howard-Evans describes his work for the firm of Cooper and Tanner, estate agents and auctioneers.

At one point, when we were in the market yard in the centre of Frome, we would have nothing but an egg sale, and you're talking several thousand eggs. You'd start at 10 o'clock and end at one o'clock, and that is a lot of eggs – a lot of eggs. You'd get bantam eggs and you'd get hen eggs and we'd get goose eggs. And goose eggs were enormous things that would sell at 50 pence each towards the end, you know. The eggs were bought by private individuals, but I think a lot of them re-sold them. They would sell to people who would then hang a sign on their gate saying 'Fresh eggs for sale', and they'd re-sell them, or they'd act for a sort of little consortium.

Quintyn Howard-Evans

Man in the Black Swan yard

The 1923 Cheese Show

Grove Hill Farm, Marston Road, demolished 1979. Drawing by Isabel George

People understand why the market moved out to Standerwick in 1990, but still lament the impact of the move on the town and the severing of that important link with the countryside. And of course the Cheese Show also moved out of town in 1999.

The stalls were where they are now but also they were all out among the cattle sheds. When my son Will was a small boy, it was the highlight really to go down during the holidays and see the stalls. The chaps trying to sell the stuff, they were usually rather an entertainment in themselves, which is not quite the same now. Another thing was to watch the actual auctioneering with the sheep pens and everything. It was a much busier place then. But of course it wasn't really a large enough area, so they moved out to Standerwick.

Isabel George

The railway was important in Frome, much more than it is now, and the line through to Bristol used to be very much coupled up with the market on Wednesdays. I can remember the cattle all being driven up into the trucks up on the railway. I used to go down in the holidays, I used to go down and watch.

The Frome Cheese Show used to happen on a Wednesday in September and that was on the Cheese Show Field, just off the Bath Road. That Wednesday was a school holiday so whole families used to go up there. It was massive! ***Cliff Ellis***

DECLINE AND …

Robert and Dorothy Hawker have spent their whole lives in Frome. This interview took place on the High Pavement in Catherine Hill, which used to be full of food shops.

I t used to be all hustle and bustle here Saturdays. Crowds of people walking up and down, but of course there was no supermarkets, so you used to say, 'Oh well, we'll go to Mr Farrant's and get something', George Hall's cake-shop and bread up there, there were several butcher's, so everything was more or less local. It don't look no different up and down here, but it's just different shops. Williams' the shop up at the top [of Bath Street], they used to drive pigs up and slaughter them in Winnard's slaughterhouse at the top of Whittox Lane.   **Robert Hawker**

Robert Hawker

Moore's in Christchurch Street West is the last of a number of shops in the town that used to serve rural needs. Ernest Clothier runs the shop.

T he shop was built in about 1923, and internally has never been touched. The Moores that were here before, they sold their larger business in 1968 so really all that was left when we came was the shop. In the 1970s we were so busy it was unbelievable. The three of us'd work in the shop and we'd never speak to one another all day long.

Our customers were farmers, cottagers, people that'd got allotments, people that keep pets. The buses used to come from Maiden Bradley and the villages, and probably half the bus would queue up to be served. We used to get farmers dropping in from market, they'd probably have a hundredweight of early potatoes and four hundredweight of maincrop to give the workers on the farm. That's the sort of trade we had. The market going out of town certainly made a big difference because farmers go to market and get what they want there, and they disappear back home. They won't come back to Frome. Sign of the times.   **Ernest Clothier**

Ernest Clothier

Quintyn Howard-Evans

Fishmonger washing fish in the leat in Cheap Street

Quintyn Howard-Evans works as an estate agent and has a professional interest in the future of shopping in Frome.

Half of my job was selling Frome, let alone selling the houses, you know. Outsiders would come here and even Cheap Street was half empty, Catherine Hill was two-thirds empty, and it just wasn't happening as a town. And at that point, there was a lot of criticism directed at the Town Council, in not allowing the chains. They were perceived as being the solution to our problems. Looking back now, it's very good they didn't come, because although we've got some big chains in there, the individuality of the shops, and the vibrancy of the shops, represent – for me – the individuality and the vibrancy of the town, which has attracted people because of that very nature.

I also don't want to live in a town that only has rows of second-hand and antique shops. I'm a great fan of it, but the town has to have proper employment too. It has to have a variety of shops and a diversity of people. It cannot become a museum-piece, and you cannot allow people to come into the town and change the nature of the town to its detriment, and you have to allow the quirkiness of the town to exist. What attracts people in the first place is its individuality but, unless people vote with their wallets, unless people use the record shop, the local greengrocer or the local health food shop, they won't survive. It isn't enough to say, 'We don't want a supermarket', you have to say, 'If the supermarket comes, we aren't going to spend all our money there'. Frome has a vibrancy that you just can't buy.

Quintyn Howard–Evans

Photograph courtesy of Getty Images

TRADERS' SECRETS – A RESTAURANT

Margaret Vaughan arrived in Frome in 1968 and opened the Settle Restaurant in Cheap Street in 1975. It had previously been the Flora Café. Her daughter, Jude, now runs La Strada Café in Cheap Street.

Margaret Vaughan

I am a shepherdess really by trade. I don't think I ever thought about why people live in a town. But in those days there used to be a shop at the top of Cheap Street where they sold the materials for the school uniform and I was going up there and I saw this place for sale. It was all run down and the posters were curled over in the windows.

I had the audacity to go into the estate agents, which I had never been in in my life. And I said, 'Have you got any details of the Flora Café?' and she came back with the keys. I had no money to buy it. And I went in and it had been empty for 18 months, two years and it was overrun with rats and mice and it was a vast property.

The solution was to lease the premises.

The Flora Café
in Cheap Street

And so the Settle was born. I tried to think of names. But, before that, and long before I'd got that far, I called the family to dinner. And I cooked this wonderful meal and I hadn't said anything at all and we all sat down together. And, I said, 'I've got some news for you'. And my husband was at the far end of the table and went on eating. And I said, 'Um, I've got a restaurant'. And there was an absolute silence. And my son said, 'Are there any more potatoes?'. How lovely! And that's how the family were introduced to the Settle and then I had to introduce Frome to the Settle. **Margaret Vaughan**

TRADERS' SECRETS – THE CHARITY SHOP

Judith Loughlin

Judith Loughlin is the manager of the Barnardo's shop in the Kingsway Precinct, where she has worked since 1988, although she remembers when it first started in Catherine Hill in 1975.

Most people don't realise the amount of work that happens behind the scenes in a charity shop. It is physically very, very hard work. You're lifting eight kilo bags constantly. You're managing a staff of volunteers, so you've got to make sure that the volunteers want to work for you, and make it fun so that they don't mind not being paid. It wasn't very easy being 31 and having to tell women in their sixties and seventies what to do. The standards weren't so rigorous and it wasn't anywhere near as professional as it has to be now.

Frome's grown enormously over the past 25 years, and the kind of people that live in Frome have changed enormously as well. We were a very working-class town then, with big factories that employed most of the working-class population of the town. People – young mums, mature ladies – came in looking for cheap clothes. It was kind of pile it high and sell it cheap then. But now charities have to invest a lot of money because they're more dependent on what comes from the high street.

It's absolutely amazing what comes in in the bags, you never know from one day to the next. Oh, a mouse, a live mouse, came in once. I looked down and there was this mouse sat, so we liberated it. It's very sad when you see people on the Antiques Roadshow and they say, 'I got this for 50p at a charity shop' and then they're going to sell it for two thousand pounds – why don't they give the charity back some of the money they sell it for? Because the charity helped them find it and we are working to help young people and their families up and down the country.   ***Judith Loughlin***

Clocking On

TEXTILES

HOUSTON'S

Daisy Bane left school at 14 and went to work selling up the looms at Houston's cloth factory, a firm long gone, but remembered in the name of a Frome road – Houston Way.

I was a pattern-warper and my sister Melinda, she was a pattern-weaver. We went to the School of Art to learn our trade. Of course you had your pattern, and you had to read your pattern, but I can't remember the patterns! I couldn't read one, not now. It was very hard, mind, but I soon got into it. Every colour had a number. There was always one number I remember. That was 896 and that was Air Force blue. I always remember that number, I don't know why.

Daisy Bane

It was skilled work, preparing the looms for the weavers. It was a jolly place to work, with singing and sweets, and a sympathetic foreman, Alec Copley, whose wife made Daisy's confirmation dress.

Inside Houston's warping shed with Daisy's foreman, Alec Copley, on the far right

49

ENGINEERING

COCKEY'S

John Stocker

John Stocker left school and went to work at Cockey's in Garston Road in 1946. His father, Bill Stocker, drove the overhead crane in the foundry, tipping red hot metal into the casts.

I was always good at drawing and I made a plan of St John's Church. They were very pleased with it so they thought I was going to be all right to go into the draughtsman's office at Cockey.

My dad always used to take a short cut, up the railway line – that was the Frome-Radstock line – scamper up over the bank, and go in. Of course he didn't have to go all the way up the yard and clock in. And a neighbour of ours, Mr Webley, he had a wonky leg and they had to be in by six, so he'd start off about five o'clock, and he was always there on time. So he'd clock my father in, save my father walking all the way up through the yard. But they came unstuck when my father didn't turn up one day. They went through his clock card and he was clocked in. They said, 'How did you get clocked in when you're not there?'. So that upset the apple-cart.

A gasholder tank being temporarily erected on the site of Cockey's works before it was despatched

Cockey's is famous for its cast-iron lamp-posts in Frome, but products in 1946 included complete gas-holders and other items for the gas industry. Although John contracted TB and only worked at Cockey's for one year, he was able to draw a detailed plan of the yard with names of some of the workers. Here he comments on the characters of some of the foremen.

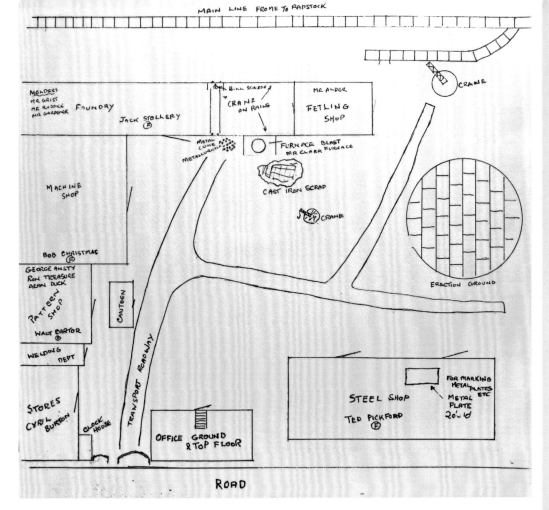

Left, John Stocker's plan of Cockey's as he remembers it in his day; above, Bill Stocker, right, at Cockey's yard

Cockey's iron works

Alan Duck [Pattern Shop] – He was my best man. And believe it or not he married a Miss Bird. Duck and Bird. Yes, lovely chap, and a beautiful carpenter.

Bob Christmas [Machine Shop] – He was one of those active people, in and out, you know, and he had a grey coat on, buttoned up, and he was rushing about all the time. And of course in there was all these different machines, lathes, milling machines. All the machines was very, very ancient and I think that was probably the reason why they went bust!   **John Stocker**

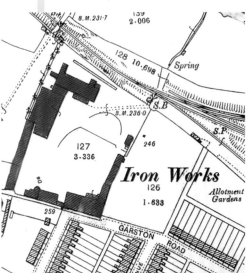

SINGER'S

© Mark Adler, Mendip Times

Jim Garrett being interviewed by Jacqueline Peverley

Singer's old factory at Cork Street

Jim Garrett worked at Singer's, Frome's famous brass foundry, and saw a gradual improvement in working conditions there. The works were just off Cork Street, right in the heart of Frome. Singer's continues to operate today in much smaller premises on the Marston Trading Estate, and the whole area west of the river and the Jenson Button Bridge has been given over to housing.

I went to work at Singer's, that would have been about 1943 I think, and that was, of course, the War years, you know. The siren would go, and we all had to move somewhere else in case they dropped a few bombs, or something. But in the event, it didn't happen, so they abandoned that idea, because it stopped the production. Making shell noses there they were, for the army, in those days. And I was an apprentice tool-maker until I was 21. I was at Singer's until 1952, and I left then, and I went and worked for Nott's, but I was only there a couple of years. And then I went back to Singer's again, so in all I worked for them over 40 years. And I was made redundant when I was 62.

Singer's was all very primitive, you know, to start with. When the shift ended and we were going home, as an apprentice I would have to go out and fill a bucket of cold water, and take it back into the workshop and put it down, and all the chaps would dive their hands in it, and wash their hands before they went home.

Singer's foundry had once been a famous maker of ornamental brass work but by the 1950s, they were making a wide variety of everyday objects, such as taps.

It was all brass fittings for houses, including Chubb keys. I made the tools that made the keys, millions of them, actually. In the press shops, they put a piece of red hot brass on the bottom of the die, and then would come the press, and then you'd have a key, to put it briefly!

It was quite noisy actually. In fact it affected my hearing over the years, and I finished with tinnitus, which I've got now. I can talk to you one to one, but if I'm in a crowd it's different. **Jim Garrett**

Furnaces next to the presses inside the factory at Singer's old site, Cork Street

Steve Francis began at Singer's as an apprentice and is now senior design engineer with the firm.

I had already done some work at the Technical College with lathes and that sort of thing but the moment we entered the press shops it was just another world. The noise was horrendous, the smell was amazing because I didn't really know what they were doing at the time but they were forging glass components in steel dies and virtual presses. I mean they had no friction and hydraulic presses in the press shops and every time the two dies came down and made a casting they took the brass casting out and swabbed it with a greasy rag. These operators were just swabbing it top and bottom and these dies were hot and there was all that greasy lubricant on it, so that was steamed off as well.

Steve Francis

Staff at Singer's from the 1950s or 1960s

So, you had this hot greasy smell of the lubricant and also the hot smell of the glass because they were heating the glass until it was cherry red in small furnaces next to the presses. And then the presses were hammering down, operated by a foot pedal, and it would come hammering down, bang! Then up again and you had all this noise and it was really dark. You walked into this place and it seemed pitch black with just the furnaces glowing next to each of the presses and I just thought, whatever have I walked into?

Steve Francis

Not all apprentices stayed with the firm for life, as Rodney Clarke and Robert Latchem point out.

Rodney Clarke

We started at Singer's almost the same day, in the late 1950s, as trainee draughtsmen. I think we were a bit overawed, because it was a big firm. I think they used to employ 600 to 800 people. We started in the only little bit that's left, in that block, we started up there. A long staircase up, and a long staircase down into the factory. Where the shops are, that was part of the tool-room, where they used to make all the dies, and I think we were in the one with the big window up on the top. It was the drawing office we went into. **Rodney Clarke**

Rodney had asthma and left after four years for a more open-air job, as a delivery driver for Express Dairies, but Robert stayed on longer.

I stayed in Singer's. They had a die-casting department, which was a very new innovation, casting brass, and I stayed in that department until I left. But I was doing draughting work for a guy on the side, and the money I was making there went past anything I could get at Singer's. So I left then and went into that structural steel side of everything.

That was a whole big new thing really. I was self-employed and worked from a bedroom at home for ages. Serious money, which makes life a bit easier. People came to me after a while and said, 'Can you do this, can you do that?'. There were several people I could work for so I went with the one that was paying the best money at the time. All very local things, three or four factories up on the trading estate. It was all happening then. We did the first supermarket on Gibraltar.

Robert Latchem

Robert Latchem

Richard Withey, born in 1970, is the third generation of Singer's workers. His grandfather started there in 1900, and his father in 1936. Yet he acknowledges that this kind of heavy manual work may now be a thing of the past.

Singer's female workers in 1978 at a time of £1 million investment in the firm

I finished school in May 1986 and started in Singer's in July. I originally went there to try and be a tool-room apprentice. I didn't get the job, but they offered me a job as a setter in the clipping machine shop. So I thought, you know, it seemed like a good idea at the time, 16, no money. I heard it through my dad, and he got me the papers at work, and that. It was quite common, then, getting work with your dad, but it's not now, I wouldn't want my children working there. I'm sure there's other things out there better paid, better lifestyle, easier to do. I mean, it's all computers now.

In the machine shop, Singer's staff celebrate the firm's 150 years with their 'JWS' engraved paperweights designed by Frome College

I suppose you could class it as a comfort zone. I know what I'm doing, I'm quite comfortable with what I do. You know I find it relatively easy, or, you know, some things are sort of challenging when you get a new tool or different jobs or stuff. I mean, three years ago we had a brand new machine put in with robots, virtually automated machine, which I found quite interesting, and I quite like using that one. I think that's the way forward, or looks to be the way forward.

Obviously the manning levels are considerably less than what they used to be. I mean, we've only got maybe 10, 12 people on our shift. Whereas when I first started, there was 100 down on Cork Street. When we moved up there, obviously a lot of them went, redundancy and that. And then you've got, what, more about 80 people across the site, now. And that's across all three shifts and the offices. I mean, from the department I was in at Cork Street, there's only two of us left, two people.

Richard Withey

Simon Giles, the youngest person in this book, represents that new and rather different lifestyle. He is a Bath man who got a job as a result of an advertisement in the Bath Chronicle *for an 'office trainee'. He is now commercial manager at the firm, a small subsidiary of a vast multinational firm called Tyco. Rather to his surprise, he found himself working with molten metal on day one.*

Simon Giles

In bulk melt, which is basically an area where we buy in scrap, we run scrap material of any type, we melt it down in huge furnaces, and then it produces brass ingots. So I had to start off in the rough and ready end, and I was working in that department. I was doing metal analysis on my very first day, and on the bus home, I remember very clearly, I thought, 'I absolutely hate this'. But as that first week went by, I did different things, met different people, and I trained in all the different departments for about six or eight months. I think it was going around the different departments and learning everything there was to know about the business at that time, whilst still doing some training in the sales office, then I got to enjoy it more. The more you did of it, the more you learned about it, and the more you realised that, at the end of the day, I wasn't going to be stuck by that furnace every single minute of the day, because I realised that it was very diverse.

Simon also reflects on the way Singer's had diversified from a firm famous for brass artwork. Their main product now is sprinklers, linked to fire-alarms, for buildings.

When I started in 1992, the biggest product line we were selling at that time, and I remember one sale item, was for water meters. We were making sprinklers, obviously, though it wasn't as big as it is today. We were making pump parts for showers, shower bodies, pipe clips, heat exchanges, bath furniture and switch plates for the wall, brass switch plates. Pretty much anything and everything you can imagine that could be made in brass, we were making it. Some of my favourite pieces were things like a saxophone mouthpiece in brass. We made a circumcision clamp for a company in America. If you wanted it made in brass, then there's a very good chance that we could make it in brass. **Simon Giles**

Tyco's premises on the Marston Trading Estate

WESSEX ENGINEERING

Bill Ellis

The entrance to Nott's Industries in Merchants Barton

Although Bill Ellis later became well known as the owner of a hardware store in Badcox – the shop currently run by his daughter called 'Country Living' – he began his working life at his father's firm, Wessex Engineering. The family came to Frome when Nott's Industries relocated to the old Silk Mill in Merchants Barton. Bill's father was a foreman at Nott's but in the 1930s he set up a separate business known as Wessex Engineering, with initially just three employees.

My father used to go out putting electric lights in for people. Father was able to wire them up an electric light which was something special for a lot of people. And I know as a kid I used to be taken along if he wanted a hand. That was my apprenticeship, I suppose. During that period I was always encouraged to come down and watch what was being done. I became a Saturday boy. If there was any odd jobs to be done, I was the one to do it. Even as a kid I was always up to my neck in oil and grease.

Bill left school at the beginning of the Second World War and worked alongside his father at Wessex while he waited to join the RAF. The jobs were 'second nature' to him. After the war he got a job as a fitter with British Road Services (BRS), repairing lorries. But he thinks his father got him the sack in order to get him back into Wessex!

Wessex had got into making parts for the laboratory side of the quarrying and roadstone industry. It was then being sold worldwide. Father retired and eventually he died. My brother had come into the firm with me and we were running it together, but to be quite honest we didn't get on very well together. I sold my share of the Wessex. That left me coming up 50, and with the bit of money I came up with I started a hardware shop with my wife Pat – we were a good pair together! – which then took me on until I was 70, which brought me very nicely into retirement. **Bill Ellis**

NOTT'S INDUSTRIES

Jim Wykes was born in Whatley in 1937 and still lives in the village. He spent his whole working life at Nott's, a small private firm at Merchants Barton, next door to Wessex Engineering and Beswick's, that employed some 60 people in its heyday.

Jim Wykes when an apprentice at Nott's in the 1950s

I was 15 when I left school. The Youth Employment people sent me to Nott's who took me on six months' trial to become a toolmaker. I was successful in the trial and then I started a five-year apprenticeship. I worked in the tool and the press shop because we had to service the tools on the presses sometimes. We went to the Technical College one day a week at the top of Park Road. After I'd finished my apprenticeship, I had to do two years' National Service in the Royal Engineers and then I went back to Nott's and stayed there until 1998 when I retired. Most of the other firms you had to stay on one machine, but at Nott's you could work all the machines and work in the press shop and do almost everything yourself. There was more variety in the job.

In the early days their main product was the Carley floats, which were used extensively during the war. As the demand for the floats died down, they went more into producing metal pressings, which were mostly in those days car parts, because there was a big boom in the car industry in the 1960s.

We had a new lathe delivered and while they were jacking it down onto the floor they allowed the whole thing to fall over and smash all the front of it up! That was one of the amusing events. I don't think the management thought it was amusing, mind! **Jim Wykes**

Carley floats

Inside the tool room at Nott's Industries

Muriel Chapman

*Female workers at
Butler and Tanner, 1937*

PRINTING

BUTLER AND TANNER

Butler and Tanner is the most famous printing firm in Frome – but not the only one. Printing was almost exclusively a male job, but women were employed in the bindery and offices. Muriel Chapman, born in 1913, is the oldest person in this book, and started work at Butler and Tanner in 1929. She worked not in the bindery itself, but in baling up the books ready for storage in the warehouse. Like many women of her era, she stopped work when she got married, and found other channels for her energy.

I was between the printing and the warehouse. The women used to sew the books and then I used to bale them up. I worked at Butler and Tanner for eight years, then I got married. That was that, we didn't work in those days. So I started the Young Wives group at St John's Church. We had quite a good gathering each month, about 25. None of them went to work so they were glad to go somewhere where there was a crèche. The Mothers' Union was the crèche to the St John's Young Wives. They were absolutely marvellous. **Muriel Chapman**

Dorothy Hawker also worked at Butler and Tanner between school and marriage.

I left school at 15 and went to Butler and Tanner, and worked till I was 20. Of course we got married just after, and then I left to bring up our son. I done several jobs, on the gathering machine in the bindery, and that was your general thing, in the bindery. We had a man overseeing the machinery, and there was about four or five of us on this

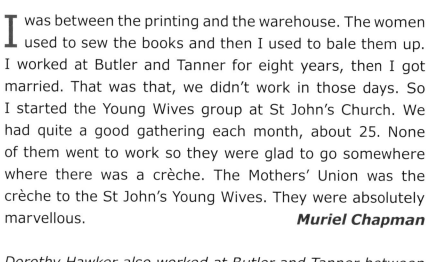

gathering machine. The men done mainly the machine maintenance, made sure they were working all right. There were good times and bad, like all jobs, but on the whole it was pretty good.

Bad times included ...

When the machine used to break down and we used to have to do the work by hand. Or the overseer didn't think we were working fast enough, and told us to hurry up, them sorts of things.

And the good times?

It was nice, all the girls together. We had quite a lot of fun. We used to go on days out with the firm. They used to have Christmas dances, and different things we used to all go to.   **Dorothy Hawker**

As at Singer's, it was common for several generations of the same family to work at the firm. Pete Stone was born in 1958, his father Ron in 1919, but Ron's father had also worked there.

[Ron] When I got demobbed in 1946 I went to work at Butler and Tanner's, at the Selwood Road works. I worked on the printing press, doing the proof copies to be sent out rough to the publisher, before they were actually put on the machine and printed in book form. I was happy as a sandboy down there. But I really got in down there because my dad had worked down there after the First World War, so that helped a bit. We had two daughters worked down there as well, Jenny and Jill. A sister-in-law worked down there, and I had one, two aunties worked down there. My wife Eileen had an aunty, so it was a family affair at the time!

Selwood Printing Works.

MACHINE DEPARTMENT.

(APPRENTICES.)

ANNUAL DINNER

AT THE Ship Inn.

Chairman :
MR. J. E. BATTEN.

Vice-Chairman :
MR. F. H. PETERS.

Above, Selwood Print Works annual dinner programme

Below, the former Selwood Road premises at the time of the Trinity demolition

Ron and Pete Stone

The former Selwood Print Works up for sale before conversion to flats

© Mendip District Council

[Pete] I tried for a job, an apprenticeship, and got one so I thought, 'Oh, I'll take it', because it had a good reputation, B and T's, good pay and all that, and you thought it was a job for life then. I liked the people, workmates, we always had a good laugh. The work I enjoyed, because it was kind of physical but not too physical! I disliked working nights. Not a lot I disliked really, up until the last couple of months it was brilliant. In 2007 another firm took over Butler and Tanner, and we knew it didn't look like it was going to last. It was pretty depressing then.

[Ron] Me dad taught Donald Tanner to drive, that would be 1922/23. Me dad started there, he'd been in the War and got wounded and he'd come home and they put him on munitions in Sheffield till the War finished. Then he came home, and the chapel he went to was Sun Street Chapel. And seeing how he could drive, one of the managers who attended Sun Street said to me dad, 'You can drive, Bert, Butler and Tanner's are buying a lorry. Would you like a job there driving?'. So me dad said, 'Yes', and the lorry they got for him was a solid tyred lorry called a Garner and the number was Y198. And me dad, because of all that, taught Donald Tanner, who was the up-and-coming one, to drive and got quite friendly with him. He bought a big American car that he used to park in Castle Street.

And me dad said to him, 'You're going to get killed before you finish, sir, with all this speed'. 'No', he said, 'I shan't, Stone. I'm getting fed up with cars, they're not fast enough, I'm going to buy an aeroplane'. And he bought an aeroplane. And he came over Frome one Sunday morning, just as I came out of church with me dad. Me dad looked and said, 'Oh, that's Donald Tanner going over'. They went to land at Bristol and they got killed. I can well remember being up Vallis Way on the morning of the funeral when all the firm lined up behind the coffin with their bowler hats on, all dressed up, and took him down and he was buried at Trinity, and in memory of him Mrs Tanner, who lived in Vallis Way, bought the first X-ray unit for the Frome Victoria Hospital. That's how Mr Humphrey Tanner, Donald's cousin, came to take over the firm as Managing Director. Humphrey was Joe Tanner's father, the last boss we had down there. **Ron and Pete Stone**

Russell Milne, born in Edinburgh in 1935, worked in the print industry in Edinburgh and in East Anglia before moving down to Frome.

I moved to Frome to Butler and Tanner's, but I left in 1985. My face did not fit, not one little bit did it fit in Butler and Tanner's. I got on very well with Joe Tanner, who was another intelligent print company owner you could talk to on an intelligent level, but unfortunately he gave the reins to others who were not as good as he was. He was a master craftsman. Everything he did, when he set the type and printed it, it was perfect. When he printed something it was an exhibition of printing. And he saved old printing machines, the very old ones, rosewood and brass, and he had a museum in his home. A brilliant man, he was the first man in that company to get a computer – and understand it. **Russell Milne**

Gerald Franks was another former employee ...

I started work at Butler and Tanner in 1945 when I was 14, at Frome Selwood Printing Works in Selwood Road, which is now flats. There used to be metal stairs outside to go into the works. You didn't clock in, you had a disc with a number on and you dropped that in when you were going in in the morning. If you were late, the desk was closed and they'd collect tuppence off you for being late.

He completed an apprenticeship as a 'comp', compositor, setting up metal type. Mistakes were costly, and an army of 'readers' would pore over draft copies of books. Last-minute corrections had to be done on the actual printing machines.

Joe Tanner

Russell Milne

Gerald Franks

The corrections were done by the compositor. The manager there at that time was Mr Bert Larkham, and he knew what you were doing all the time. For late corrections you had to do what was called a 'machine revise'. When you do a machine revise you don't take the forms off the machine. You had to crawl on the machine and do these corrections by hand, because it was all set up on the machine and all locked in the machine.

The wartime had been very disruptive for B&T.

Butler and Tanner's site at Adderwell, known as Adderwell Works

The bindery and other machines went to Bath because they used Butler and Tanner's premises at Adderwell for manufacturing aeroplanes in the war. When they eventually moved all the big machines back down to Adderwell after the war, we used to have to cycle to do a machine revise from Selwood down to Adderwell. You had to pick up the type you wanted, make sure you had enough, and then cycle down to Adderwell and do the revise, and then come all the way back again!

All printers belonged to trade unions. There were different unions for different crafts and trades, though gradually over the years they were all absorbed into the GPMU and now Unite.

Relations were very good between management and workforce in them days. There was no big hassle at all really. I mean, different union matters used to get settled in the works. **Gerald Franks**

In 2007, Butler and Tanner was bought up by a firm called Media Print Investment (MPI) headed by Mike Dolan. The relationship did not prosper, and all staff were made redundant by a letter delivered on a Saturday morning in April 2008. On May 23, workers from B&T paraded through Frome from North Parade to the B&T factory in Caxton Road via the Market Place.

Butler and Tanner workers march through Frome in May 2008 after mass redundancies were announced

Stuart North was Father of the Chapel [a senior trade union representative] at that time. Eventually, the firm was rescued by the intervention of publisher Felix Dennis, and is now called Butler Tanner & Dennis.

I thought it was important to get the message out to the local community about what was going on with one of the town's biggest and best employers. I was right at the front of the demonstration, and as we got down into the town, there were shoppers applauding, and there were

Joseph Tanner, who was taken into partnership with W.T. Butler in 1863 to form the printing house of Butler and Tanner

shop-workers coming out and cheering and congratulating us, you know, lending their support. It was very successful, we had huge support from the town, we all stuck together, the employees and the families, we had fund-raising evenings to help those that had really suffered.

As a printing company, we had produced one or two of Felix Dennis' books, because he is a poet amongst other things. I think he was saddened to hear of the closure of the last high quality, full colour, book printer in the UK of its kind. Felix Dennis is a businessman at the end of the day and he saw potential in Butler and Tanner as a business, going forward. He's a very generous man and he does an awful lot for charity, but he's also a very shrewd businessman. B&T[&D] has to stand on its own two feet in the future.

Stuart North

Butler Tanner & Dennis staff in the factory at Caxton Road

D.R. HILLMAN AND CO

Cliff Ellis's mother and father were both in the print business. His father had moved to Frome in the 1920s to work for Butler and Tanner, where his mother worked too. Later she worked for D.R. Hillman and Co., lithographic printers.

Donald Hillman set up with one printing machine in that area I call 'under the archway' at the lower end of Keyford, opposite the fire station. He had one large printing machine and one printer and that's how he started. Gradually he expanded, but my mother used to have delivered to the house the large printed sheets and she would hand fold them so they would be in the sections that made up books. In those days books were stitched at the backs and obviously you print up sheets like 64-page or 128-page or even 256-page, and then they fold to be in order.

So my mother was effectively Donald Hillman's 'process end' of the printing, because that was her trade. I remember him coming to the house many an evening with like 250 sheets they'd had printed and wanted them folded up that night. She worked on the dining table. And then they expanded and expanded and he created a whole department which she then ran with about eight other women. So she gathered them in for him, from her past. They'd all been trainees with her at Butler and Tanner's, but they retired, had families and so on. They worked part time, 9am to 11.30am, and then went back at 1.30pm to 5pm. **Cliff Ellis**

Hillman Print Works 1962 Frome Carnival entry, Snow in Frome

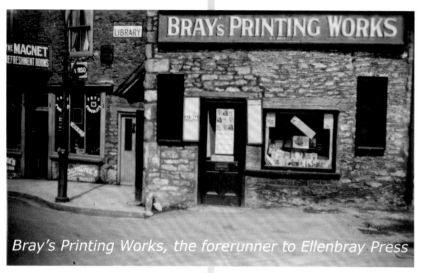
Bray's Printing Works, the forerunner to Ellenbray Press

The George Hotel

Reproduced by permission of English Heritage

ELLENBRAY PRESS

Alan Fairhurst began his working life at Ellenbray Press. Elllenbray's is now a stationer's and toyshop in the Westway precinct, in the fine building that was once Frome Library. The Angel pub is now called the Archangel.

I started off with Ellenbray Press, which was a printing company. Where the Job Centre is now there used to be a big wooden hut, and it used to be in there. I started off life as an apprentice there and I was there for six or seven years.

I was 21 and I was working part-time at the George Hotel as barman and it was taken over, and they persuaded me, and said, 'Would you like to become trainee manager?'. Well, I was fed up with the printing industry because we were on strike every 12 weeks or so in those days, every little dispute, everyone was out on strike. So I said, 'Yes, I'll take it on'. I lived above the George because although I lived in Frome, by the time you'd finished at night and the guests had all gone to bed, it was 3 in the morning and back up at 7 in the morning to cook breakfast for the guests again. Yeah, I stayed there for quite a while. I also worked in the old Angel. ***Alan Fairhurst***

LIGHT INDUSTRY

BESWICK'S

Joan Smith, née Lyons, and Sylvia Austin both worked on the shop-floor at Beswick's, assembling fuses.

I went to Beswick's in September 1939. The job was advertised in the paper, and it all worked out. I was soldering fuses. You won't believe it but I had some solder on my hands there and that's about 40 years ago and I've still got two marks there. Sometimes we used to do the soldering and sometimes we used to do the wiring, you put the wire through the fuses.

Joan, front, and her colleagues by the solder pots at Beswick's

Beswick's was in Merchants Barton, down by the slaughterhouse. It was terrible in the mornings. They'd leave all the doors open and you'd see all the animals. Terrible! Things you don't forget. We had a lovely foreman, Mr Puttick, George Puttick. He had one arm and he had one finger off and he could tie up his own shoe laces and everything you know. I remember one day I was talking to Betty Poole. He come along and bashed our heads together. He used to say, 'Lyons', and I'd say, 'Yes', and he'd say, 'I heard you talking'. I said I wasn't talking so he said, 'I heard you whistling'. I whistle all the time. Ever such a nice man he was. Couldn't wish for a better foreman. No favours. He would treat everybody the same. ***Joan Smith***

Beswick's workers outside the factory in their lunch break

We were on bonus working, doing the fuses, and of course the more fuses you could push out, the more money you earned. It was quite nice. I worked with a lot of Italian girls at the time. They had music playing which was good. In those days you could take your own records in and the office girls would play them through the loudspeakers

A pack of fuses made at Beswick's

so that it came through to the factory. We used to play Elvis, the old Fifties music, the old Sixties music, rock-and-roll music. If it was somebody's birthday we'd all go to the pub and have a drink of a lunchtime.

Our daughter Debbie was born in September 1962. I didn't go to work straightaway but I started down Beswick's in that very bad winter, 1962/63. Because Tony was off work, he couldn't get to work on building sites because of the bad weather, so I took a job at Beswick's. Some friends of Tony's from Batcombe moved to Frome, they were lovely people. Every morning, I used to get up, put Debbie in the pram and push her in all that ice and snow up to Sheppards Barton, drop her off, and then go on to work at Beswick's. And the same in the evening.

Sylvia Austin

The all-female shop floor workers in the main shop at Beswick's

Gloria Wingrove, née Jones, born in 1950, was doing well at school, especially at maths, but still left at the first opportunity when she was 15.

Gloria's 1966 contract for employment at Beswick's

Well, I got a little bit of pressure from my mum and the headmaster – they wanted me to stay on at school but all my friends were leaving and going to Woolworth's so I defied them and I went to Woolworth's for a year. At the time there was a Mr Mitchell who used to be the boss there and I think because he had a daughter himself who worked there, we always got spoiled! But when he retired, the new one didn't like the young ones so within two weeks we all went round to Beswick's then, all 10 of us.

After several takeovers, a USA-based firm, Cooper Bussmann, moved production to China.

I finished there in 2001 and that's when it all went to China. It was ever so hard because we were like one big family most of us there. We'd been there so long, everybody got on so well and we just loved doing what we done. It was just a dream place to work really. It was only the last few years when Bussmann took it over it all started changing. Suddenly it was triple shifts and then more and more automation came in so you couldn't actually speak the whole time you were there. And it was so noisy that you couldn't have a conversation. But when I first went there, there was about a dozen of you sat either side of a long bench. It was all hand-assembled so really it was like a social club but you managed to get some work done as well.

Gloria Wingrove

Dawn Chapman

A Beswick worker's 'family' made before the firm's closure in 2001

Dawn Chapman shared Gloria Wingrove's sense of Beswick's as a family, and before the factory closed they made life-size puppet figures to put in one of the empty workshops. She went to work at Beswick's from school and quickly became a supervisor, and later worked in personnel. When the firm closed down, she found herself in charge of redundancy scheduling.

The first round of redundancies came in the mid-1990s, and led to great changes in production, changes complicated by the cramped nature of the factory site. 80 workers lost their jobs. Of Cooper Bussmann's production move to China, she says:

I remember that being quite a painful time because it was like being part of a huge family. It didn't really matter who went. You didn't want anybody to go, and on the Friday there was a letter produced for ever single member of staff and it was just whether you opened your letter and you were safe or you weren't, really. For some it was heartbreaking. It was almost like at that point there was no opportunity to say goodbye and it was so sad. There was no event that you could put on which would lessen that blow. It was not sudden. It was a big reality check and everybody was aware that something was going on and something had to change, something was going to give.

We had the announcement of the closure in September 2000, so we were given a year's notice. It was completely out of the blue. There were lots of tears and lots of sadness. Fear was the biggest thing. We were explained that the business was going to be relocated to China. It wasn't anything which was callous, it was just business. We had our last day officially, when nearly everybody was finishing, in August 2001. We had a huge party, we had a barbecue and we had a bar.

Dawn Chapman

Ian Spearing

If most of the shop-floor workers at Beswick's were women, the maintenance and engineering department was almost entirely men. Ian Spearing was one of them.

I met Bill Sadler one day, who was the foreman of the Beswick's maintenance crew, and he said, 'Oh, we're looking for another carpenter, do you want to come and join us?', so I went and got the job there. So I actually spent five years with Beswick's before I went to Canada.

Ken Beswick was the actual governor, we used to call him that in those days. He was the boss of the whole thing as it was his business. Grant Beswick, his son, was the managing director and after that they had about five or eight different supervisors, male and female, because 600 women worked in that factory manufacturing fuses, that's at the time I joined. Now they had a tool room for the engineering end of the factory that manufactured the fine tools and stuff that they did the work with and then they had what we called the hut which may be still there at the back of Beswick's and that was the maintenance workshop. So in there we had a painter, an electrician, Bill who was foreman carpenter, and me and Dan Dubbins as carpenters.

Ian Spearing

Some of Ian Spearing's fellow maintenance workers at Beswick's

73

Ray Daniel

Ray Daniel worked at Beswick's from 1959 to 1966 before going to teach in a technical college.

Grant's father, Kenneth Beswick, started the firm in a garage. He and his wife sat down in the garage at the bottom of the garden and made fuses by hand and gradually got good at it and got known. They called themselves Alert Fuses. He would get things done, but he often had fallings out with his son. They used to come and have their rows in my little office on occasion and I used to sneak out because I found it terribly embarrassing. But this is only just father and son things, you know, the sort of challenge.

In a lot of ways it was a very ethical firm, I think. They weren't into cheating or profiteering in any sort of way. They wanted to do a good service. We always wanted to make our fuses the best. Quality people talk about percentage failures of items and we used to say that if somebody buys a toy or something for their kid for Christmas and it's got a fuse in it that fails, that's a 100% failure for them.

We had a branch of the firm in Exmouth which employed something like 20 maybe 30 girls, run by a very, very clever, good supervisor woman. One of the perks was that you could have a holiday in the flat, and it

Vol. I. No. 6.
Summer, 1964.

Fuse News

USE "ALERT" FUSES.
RE-FUSE ALL
SUBSTITUTES.

The
House Organ
of
K. E. Beswick, Ltd.

A 1964 copy of Beswick's in-house magazine produced for its workers

Grant Beswick, the firm's managing director, presents an apprentice with his indentures in 1978

was very nice. We weren't actually overpaid, we were never overpaid, but we could have a summer holiday there. It was a very good flat but you had to go and have a word with them in the factory and see that things were all right. I had four or five very nice holidays down there.

Ray Daniel

Beswick's male workers attend a leaving party at the Crown Hotel, 1966, for Ray Daniel, front row, seated, holding a tankard

BENCHAIRS

Benchairs (Western) Ltd
Manor Road
Frome
Somerset BA11 4BW
Direct sales line 0373 61441
Telex 449680

Advertising material from Benchairs when it was based at Marston Trading Estate

BENCHAIRS

Val Humphries worked for Benchairs, who imported chairs and other furniture, sometimes in kit form, from Eastern Europe. The firm used a number of sites in the town for assembly and as warehouses, including the old vinegar works in Park Hill Drive and the Cheese and Grain Hall, as well as a modern factory on Marston Trading Estate and a warehouse at Frome railway station. It also had a special rail wagon designed for its use.

It was a furniture manufacturing company and I started off as an office junior making the tea and doing the filing. Then I worked in the general office but I finished off in the sales department, and it was a really big company in its time. It started off in London. I was there for 28 or 29 years, and I left in 1990. I did enjoy it there, and of course we were very lucky at the time because the company had moved from London and we were on very good money because what they were earning in London they brought down with them.

I liked it in the sales department. We used to reckon we could sell snow to the Eskimos at that time, which now I can see is probably pretty annoying because you pick up the phone umpteen times a day and somebody is trying to flog you something and I'm saying, 'I don't, I'm not interested', but we were doing it all the time. We were supplying perhaps a thousand chairs at a time and in those days when you had a big board in the office, and if you made a really good sale, your name would go up that you'd sold 500 chairs to so and so. It was quite exciting at the time!

Val Humphries

John Stocker also worked at Benchairs.

Benchairs eventually went bankrupt in 1991, that's when I finished with them. I was there for 32 years. I started working at Park Hill Drive, Welshmill, in 1960. That was the ex-vinegar works building. The owner in them days was Mr Chapman of London. A little man with a big personality and everyone had to jump when he came. It was all brushed up, all nice and tidy, he used to come down in his big Bentley and everybody had to be on their best behaviour. He was very strict.

At Welshmill we used to have to run everywhere, there wasn't time to walk, it was so busy. The containers used to come in with 1,400 chairs on them, and we had various places dotted round Frome where we housed it. It was only later years under Mr Bayman that we used the Cheese and Grain. I was in there 10 years just stacking it up and unstacking it. It went on from strength to strength, we had some very good years under Mr Bayman. Eventually I think what was the demise of it was we used to have all our furniture come from Romania, Hungary, Yugoslavia – we never used to make it, you see. Of course when the communists started losing their power, the workers wanted more money, although I can't really speak for the management, all I was doing was loading and off-loading all the vans. **John Stocker**

Above, John Stocker carries chairs in the station warehouse

Left and below, the Cheese and Grain building in use by Benchairs

WALLINGTON WESTON

Freda Henly was born in Milk Street in 1921 and worked for Wallington Weston while the firm was still at Adderwell, the site later occupied by Cuprinol and now houses. It is described on maps of the period as an 'India rubber factory'. She stopped work when her first child was born in 1941.

I went to work in a factory called Wallington Weston. They made rubber soles for shoes. We used to have to cut round them hot rubber soles with scissors. It was hard work but there was not much work in the 1930s. They weren't always all that hot, but I can remember having to wear gloves. In my shop it was all women, but it was men who made them, and then they came up in the lift and we had to trim them. This was down at Adderwell. Cuprinol took over afterwards, but it's gone now. It was Wallington and Weston and the Westons lived in Adderwell House. There was a lot of people working at Butler and Tanner so we could walk to work with them as well. Something like you see the children from the school! The girls were very nice, we all got on well together. **Freda Henly**

Trevor Biggs went to Wallington Weston in 1972. By now it was a plastics firm in Vallis Road, where the Redrow Estate is now. He became active in both the social club and the trade union.

I'd got married in 1961 and I had the two children by then. To be honest, I couldn't afford to stay at Wilson and Scotchman any more. So I went to Wallington and Weston's as a semi-skilled maintenance fitter-welder. But there were things I could do – their skilled people never had a clue what to do, I mean, anything in copper or anything like stainless steel I could get on and do, and they recognised that after a while. Once I got trained up to the actual mechanics of the factory, I was made up on skilled rates. It was a terrific change because I was only on days for a

Freda Henly

Trevor Biggs

couple of months, and then I had to go on shifts, which I knew. And that was six weeks off, six weeks on. So it did mean me doing 6am to 2pm, 2pm to 10pm, then nights, through the weekend, so it was a big change. It was a good move financially but it was a big culture change.

I was a shop steward for 25, 26 years. I did get pushed into it, of course, as everybody does! I suppose I was too responsible to let just anyone do it but I wished someone

else had done it. I still thought there was a lot of injustice that wasn't being looked at. You can't expect a huge rise in money if you're not going to do something to earn it. If you want more then I always thought you needed to give more.

Trevor Biggs

Women workers at Wallington Weston canteen

Sylvia Austin had worked at Beswick's and at Benchairs. Wallington Weston was a subsidiary of Marley and made sheets of Marley flooring, tiles and sliding doors.

I left that for a better job at Wallington Weston and I was up there for about seven years. That was in the tile department, sorting out the tiles as they came off the machine. They came down on a conveyor belt and the girls at the bottom had to sort the tiles out, the ones that were no good we'd just fling behind us into a bin! It was a lovely job, that was the best job I had, up there. It was good money. What I liked about it, you'd start at half-past seven in the morning but on a Friday you'd finish at one o'clock so you had a nice long weekend.

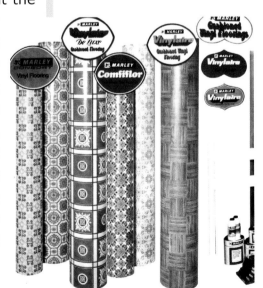

The men were mainly on making the vinyl. The women were in the door department and the tile department, that was the women's jobs. There was a union up there and that was brought up many a time. We did go on strike in the Seventies. I think we did have pay rises, we earned good money in the end.

Sylvia Austin

Georgina Phillips

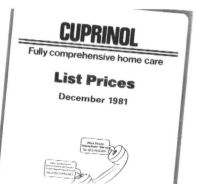

CUPRINOL
Fully comprehensive home care

List Prices
December 1981

CUPRINOL

Georgina Phillips, who was born in 1935, had worked for Roads Reconstruction on leaving school. When her son was 10 years old, and her husband out of work, she found a job close to her home on the Mount Estate. Cuprinol made wood preservatives.

I went to the Labour Exchange and they gave me a green card for Roads Reconstruction at Garston. So I called in there and had an interview for credit control in the accounts department, and then on the way home I passed Cuprinol and I thought, 'I could try Cuprinol, that's quite near where I live'. So I went in and asked and strangely enough they had a vacancy in their credit control department! And I had an interview straight away. So I came home and thought, 'Well, I've just got to wait'.

In the event, she received a phone call asking her to start the next Monday, the beginning of a long association with the firm which lasted until her retirement in 1996. Computers had arrived in industry, not the laptops and PCs that we know today, but giant mainframe machines with their special rooms and staff.

I started in the credit control department, but times had changed so much. All of a sudden, instead of your ledger sheets, it's become a computer printout. We had a computer room but you weren't allowed to know anything about what happened in the computer room. That was like a code room. You weren't able to do anything yourself. If you wanted something printed you had to contact the computer room.

A vacancy arose in the purchasing department and I applied for it and got the job. There again, it was just starting at the beginning and learning. It was a very small department. My boss had made his way up from being in the works. We purchased everything for the whole firm.

Georgina Phillips

It Wasn't All Work

SOCIAL LIFE

Ian Spearing's band 'The Modernaires' played for dances at the George Hotel, in the ballroom [on what is now the first floor of the adjoining Nat West bank]. Occasionally things got out of hand.

*The Modernaires
Dance Band in 1955*

B ut once we had a terrible fight in the George Hotel. It was the thing to be in the paper. There was a crew up there, I can't remember the name but one of them was a boxer and he was well known in Frome in those years. That would be in the middle Sixties then. And there was another guy who was supposed to be in there who was going with his girlfriend or something, I don't know the whole story, but they had warned the people on the door that there may be trouble if this boxer turned up. So anyway, whatever happened, they were not on the door when he came in.

But anyway, this fight started and apparently this guy sat out there or whatever it was with his hands in his pockets and this boxer came through the door and just punched him in the face and knocked him down and a fight started outside the ballroom. But what happened was, as they got more raucous and they broke through the doors into the ballroom they started to bang into the dancers. Well, it was late on in the evening and most dancers were a little bit inebriated and they didn't want to be banged, so they turned round and clobbered the guys you see and it started a mass fight. And you've never seen the likes of it. One of them ran down and got the beat cop that was down in the Market

The Coronets, Ian Spearing's last band in the UK, perform at the George Hotel in 1966

Place. He came up the stairs and he never got in the door 10 feet before his helmet was across the floor. Anyway, all my band got up and stood behind me by the window and I'm now in front and nobody's going to damage my drums I can tell you, after the expense. All the women are standing on the seats and there's bodies flying all over the place and there's one coming at me and I just caught him before he fell into my drums and pushed him back out.

But when the thing was over the dance finished and we went up to the police station and drove by it and they had all the arrested people stood outside because they didn't have enough room to put them in. It was lines of them, all lined up with cops stood all around them.

Ian Spearing

Gerald Franks worked at Butler and Tanner but also as a special constable at busy times in the town. The Hexagon Club was a night club at the back of the Memorial Theatre, in what is now called the Assembly Rooms.

I worked weekends mainly, or carnival days. Police don't do carnival days now but we used to do all the duties on carnivals and the Cheese Show. Carnival day we were always busy. Then sometimes you were on duty on a Friday night, a Saturday night, when the Hexagon was going. We used to park up Park Road in a police car for people coming out the Hexagon at night. It was a night club, dance club, and now and again used to get a little bit of trouble. I used to go on at say 10 o'clock at night and finish about 2 o'clock in the morning. **Gerald Franks**

The Hexagon Club in its heyday

Beswick's workers inside the factory at Christmas 1998

Dawn Chapman worked at Beswick's.

I'm still very good friends with everybody. We're all good friends and when we get together now, we often say that we were 19, 20, 21 years old and we'd never earned so much money in our life. We worked hard and we played hard, all of us. Even on a late shift we would all take our clothes in on a Thursday night and Friday night. We'd clock out at 10 and we'd go in the toilets and all get changed and we'd all go to the Hexagon and then we'd meet in the morning for coffee before we started on the half-eleven shift. At that time that was our kind of disco. So we'd go out together and we'd go home to eat and sleep and then go to work again. I think Frome was aware when the Beswick girls were on a night out by the volumes of us!

Dawn Chapman

Dorothy Hawker worked at Butler and Tanner as a young woman.

I t was nice, all the girls together. We had quite a lot of fun. We used to go on days out with the firm. They used to have Christmas dances, and different things we used to all go to. **Dorothy Hawker**

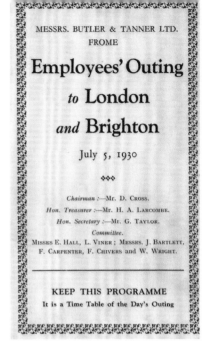

MESSRS. BUTLER & TANNER LTD.
FROME

Employees' Outing
to **London**
and **Brighton**

July 5, 1930

❖❖❖

Chairman :—Mr. D. Cross.
Hon. Treasurer :—Mr. H. A. Larcombe.
Hon. Secretary :—Mr. G. Taylor.
Committee.
Misses E. Hall, L. Viner ; Messrs. J. Bartlett,
F. Carpenter, F. Chivers and W. Wright.

KEEP THIS PROGRAMME
It is a Time Table of the Day's Outing

Above, a programme for a Butler and Tanner employees' outing, 1930

Left, Butler and Tanner Netball Club 1931

Jude Curtis was a district nurse based at Frome Medical Practice.

I 'm a great believer that if it's a tough job and you can make it fun, it makes life a lot easier, so we're all good friends. A lot of the team have been with me for a long time and I'm lucky enough to be able to interview and recruit my own staff so they are all very carefully picked and we have got a superb group of nurses. The Practice invite us to their do's and we take our other half with us and we never talk about shop. I had them all over to my house recently and all the other halfs came as well. My eldest one in the team who is 71 has just retired so we had a retirement party in my house. I haven't got a big house but it was fun. We all contributed

Jude Curtis

some food and made a really lovely evening of it and had some games. Yes, we do meet socially, not frequently but regularly.　　***Jude Curtis***

WORKS CLUBS

BUTLER AND TANNER

Both Ron and Pete Stone remember the extensive social life at Butler and Tanner.

[Ron] They had a good sports club down there with their own bowling green. A shooting club, they had a swimming section, a football section, they had a cricket section, yes, sport was quite strong down there. And skittles too. Swimming I did, quite a bit, that was always my sport, swimming. Yes, we had a good swimming section. We swam down the old Frome swimming pool in Rook Lane. The sports club used to pay for

The Caxton Club

Frome Swimming Baths in Rook Lane

us to have an hour every Saturday night, specially for Butler and Tanner's. And then when they moved to the new swimming pool, up the sports centre, we still hired it for an hour every Saturday night, but we did allow the police to come in and join with us.

[Pete] They had a canteen and they used to hire it out quite a bit for weddings, and they put a skittle alley in there. Yes, they used to have quite a lot of stuff, they had cabarets up there. Members of the public had to be signed in, if I remember right, and eventually they done it so that if you paid a fee, like a membership every year, people who didn't work down there could come in.

[Ron] You could hire it for different things as well, and I remember a lot of boxing shows were laid on down there, people from London, top boxers came in there boxing.
Ron and Pete Stone

Gerald Franks also worked at Butler and Tanner.

The Caxton Club, which was a canteen, they used to run dances, skittles down there, bingo, cabarets, all that used to go on down there. There was a bar down there as well, a proper club, and also a billiard room, and also table tennis rooms as well. I mean, there's not a lot of table tennis played in Frome now because there's nowhere for them to go, they always used to play down at Butler and Tanner's. Of course that canteen's all closed now. It's a great loss to the town. **Gerald Franks**

Members of Butler and Tanner's Lunchtime Draughts League from the 1970s

The Singer's committee at the opening of the new clubhouse in 1976

The 'Dragon Bangers', winners of the six-a-side football competition at a J.W. Singer & Sons' annual presentation evening, 1977

SINGER'S

As a large employer, Singer's had a very active social club, but when the firm moved to smaller premises on the industrial estate in 1999, the social side largely ceased. Steve Francis still works at Singer's.

From the time I joined Singer's, the social club was a major thing in the company. But for years and years they had been doing events, playing skittles, having dances, but they didn't actually have their own site. I got involved even when I was an apprentice because I have been playing skittles in Singer's ever since 1968 or 1969. But by 1976 the social club had all this money which was building up and eventually the firm allowed them to build a clubhouse on the back of the factory. They made a new car park at the back of the old factory, which is now the houses in Delta Close. Between the car park and the factory buildings there was this waste land, so the firm allowed the social club to build a clubhouse on this land.

What the firm said was that the social club could do this as long as it was run as a proper business and it made money and at no time did the firm have to lay out money to keep it going. So that was what we did and many people in Frome can remember the Colander Club. It had a main hall, a bar, a squash court, a rifle range, all built into the one complex. So you could actually raise money by hiring it out. We had a full-time manager in charge and it was run as a proper business. So the skittles became a five-night-a-week event instead of a one and we had dances and things most Saturday nights, especially through the summer, and we had professional entertainers come along.

In 1999 we were hoping we could keep it going, but the firm were selling the whole of the factory site. So they said, 'Sorry, the clubhouse is going, it has been sold'. So we lost the clubhouse.   **Steve Francis**

CUPRINOL

Like Beswick's, Cuprinol was another friendly Frome factory that no longer exists. Georgina Phillips worked in the office but it was the shop-floor workers who tended to dominate the social activities.

Yes, there was a social club. It was a wooden hut, but they had a skittle alley in there, you know. It was mostly the factory that ran the social club and were involved with it, I think.

Every Christmas they used to provide a party for all the employees' children. They had a lovely time, and they'd have a present. They must have done fund-raising through the year to have got that. Yes, it was a very thriving social club.

Georgina Phillips

Children of Cuprinol staff enjoy a New Year's party at the St John Ambulance headquarters in Bath Street, January 1969

Keith Higgins

EXPRESS DAIRIES

The creamery at Oldford still exists, although it has gone through several changes of ownership. Its busiest period was probably when it was owned by Express Dairies. Keith Higgins talks about the active social life there.

We had a very good social club there. They did a lot of things, parties and outings and took the kids to the pictures and things. There was no actual club room, so we always went somewhere else, and we had our annual dinner, Christmas dinner, at the Civic Hall in Trowbridge. There were a lot of people working there in those days before I left, I suppose about 300 at one time. It started at about 150 when I went there.

If a new film came to Frome everybody could go with their children and it was all free, paid by the social club. I remember going to the Gaumont

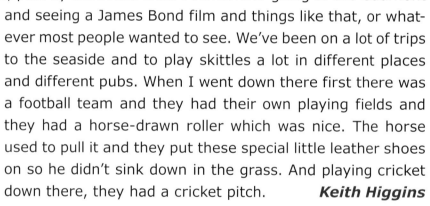

and seeing a James Bond film and things like that, or whatever most people wanted to see. We've been on a lot of trips to the seaside and to play skittles a lot in different places and different pubs. When I went down there first there was a football team and they had their own playing fields and they had a horse-drawn roller which was nice. The horse used to pull it and they put these special little leather shoes on so he didn't sink down in the grass. And playing cricket down there, they had a cricket pitch. ***Keith Higgins***

The Gaumont cinema, in Cork Street, on which site the Westway cinema now stands

WALLINGTON WESTON

As at Beswick's and Cuprinol, work at Wallington Weston was accompanied by a good social life, as Trevor Biggs recalls.

I went from a very small firm to a very big one that was backed up by Marley. It actually belonged by this time to Marley Tiles. The first few years we were up there we actually hired a train for our outings. We went to the Isle of Wight from Frome and down to Paignton and Dawlish. Then a couple of times we went, we shared, we just had so many carriages on the train. We had a wonderful social club that used to arrange the outing, not the company.

We had dances, carnival floats, there was different committees for different things. We had our own skittles league, for instance, which was run at the Ring o'Bells to start with and later The Globe. Yes, that was good.

A big party was held to celebrate Queen Elizabeth II's Silver Jubilee in 1977. At this time Wallington Weston employed 800 staff, some of them travelling into Frome from a wide area.

Marley financed a big marquee up on the Showground, even the commissionaires were allowed to come, because we had them on the doors up there. Marley actually hired commissionaires from Bristol to look after the factory while they were away. They had a live band up there and a disco, and during the afternoon, the kids had their party there.

Trevor Biggs

Workers' children meet Santa at Wallington Weston's Christmas party in 1968

BENCHAIRS

Benchairs was another firm with a well-organised and varied social life, as John Stocker recounts.

Benchairs used to organise trips all over the place – we used to go off playing skittles, things like that. We'd go down to the seaside where it was in and out of the pubs all day long, that was what most of them wanted to do. They decided after having a few drinks to take a rowing boat out. And one of them stood up to say, 'Look over there, on the horizon'. And with that he tumbled over and went into the water. He had a big thick cardigan on and he sunk out of sight! Everybody looked over the side of the boat for him. And one chap, a big chap, stuck his hand out and said, 'I think I've got his hair!'. Funnily enough this one that fell overboard had long hair, and he pulled him up, 'Yes, I've got him', and pulled him over into the boat absolutely dripping wet. You could tell exactly where they went that day because you could see this trail of water all along the pavements and into the pub. **John Stocker**

BESWICK'S

As well as going to pubs and clubs together, Beswick's had a more organised social life, based on the Phoenix Club. The owners, the Beswick family, would present cups and trophies to winning teams.

Skittles, darts, everything, yes parties. I was captain of two teams. I got two cups. Well I've got rid of the two cups but I've still got the big shields. We played darts with the Beswick's girls from the Warminster factory, but we lost by a double one. I had two teams, one was called the Spitfires and the other one the Untouchables.

Below left, Beswick's ladies' skittles team, 1966, with Mrs K. Beswick, who presented the cups, seated centre; right, staff enjoy a Beswick's works party in the early 1950s

All the [Beswick] family were friendly. They would stop and talk to you in the factory. You couldn't wish for anything better. At Christmas, we used to get a box of chocolates and Mr Beswick used to get all the family to come. **Joan Smith**

Ian Spearing worked in the maintenance department at Beswick's, and eventually emigrated to Canada, though he still visits Frome.

When I left, they had a huge farewell do at the factory and they stood me up and had all the staff down from all over, from Warminster and Exmouth, and they had all the girls in this one room and I had to go up there and stand in front of them and say 'Goodbye' to them all. It were marvellous because they all gave me a whole packet of money to buy luggage or whatever I wanted. I still have a Parker pen engraved with the time I worked there from the staff at Beswick's, and all those are nice little keepsakes.

Ken Beswick was one of the best governors in the old-fashioned style. He was very generous. At Christmas, I don't know what he did for the girls, but he always gave you an extra week's pay. You got a free turkey and a box of chocolates for your wife and if you smoked, 100 cigarettes. I wonder how many people in this day and age would do it? And he was very, very sensible. He knew you wouldn't mix men and women in the party situation and we always used to smile at that. But he would take all of us men, and I remember the last party we had down at the Portway Hotel and he'd give us a dinner and however much you wanted to drink. **Ian Spearing**

Top, skittles players celebrate one of many successes; middle, Beswick's Alert Works Football Team, in the early 1950s; bottom, female staff enjoy a night out

Butler & Tanner's 1930s entry: Milk Marketing Board Dream

Carnival 2010: with the decline of large-scale firms in Frome, most carnival floats are now built by the various Carnival Clubs in the area. In 2010 and 2011 Home in Frome took part in the Carnival to encourage small-scale, low-tech entries perhaps closer to the spirit of the early carnivals.

CARNIVAL

While many firms in Frome supported Carnival, Bill Ellis was ideally placed to use the resources of his father's firm, Wessex Engineering, to support Carnival in the years after the Second World War. His experience of working as a fitter for BRS also came in handy.

Whilst I was with Wessex, Father, he used to know people in town, and he got involved with Carnival, and if Carnival wanted something, they'd always say, 'Yes, go and see Ernie. His lad'll do whatever you want'. The firm had a nice little truck, and the wife and I used to borrow the truck and dress it up and go into Carnival. And we done quite well with this carnival float. Father always used to get the benefit of it – 'Oh, your lad done well, Ernie!'. He didn't get involved with it but he always got the praise. He liked that bit! So I was able to do things for Carnival which anybody in a job that's working for somebody wouldn't normally be allowed to do.

That went on for a bit and I suddenly got a bit ambitious, and I thought I'd go a bit bigger. I happened to know of a firm that had a 3-ton Bedford going for scrap, and I brought it in and modified it, and the thing is still going round. Now every Christmas, no

longer under my care, they've formed a trust to keep it going, it goes round with Father Christmas, nobody ever does it as a Carnival thing.

So that's something I always look back at, my days at the Wessex, the old Bedford Christmas float. I bought a second lorry to have spares, but it did involve a nice piece of 8'x4' metal plate to be cut up to make the front bumper. I was carefully cutting it up when Father come along and said, 'What's that for?'. I said, 'The float'. 'Ooh!', was the reply. Nothing else was said but 'Ooh' – I had the use of it and he paid for it from his firm.

Bill Ellis

My father, Bert Stone, used to drive the lorry on the floats. They used to meet in Welshmill Road, because there were only a few to start off with. They would all line up down Welshmill Road, come down North Parade, up round King Street, along Behind Town [Christchurch Street East], and down Bath Street and through the Market Place again.

I remember one year they had it called 'Doctors Quack'em and Kill'em'. There was a man on the back, I remember his name actually, Bill Aplin, he was a good swimmer, goalkeeper for Frome Water Polo team, and he was laid in the bed, and there were these doctors so-called, one had a mallet and the other one had a knife, called Doctors Quack'em and Kill'em. **Ron Stone**

Above, Butler & Tanner's 1930s entry: Doctors Quack'em & Kill'em; below, The Sea Hawk, a 1953 entry by Hodder & Sons

Beswick's workers pose for a photo before their carnival entry sets off from Marston Trading Estate

Carnival entries parade through the town

Daisy Bane was on the Carnival Committee for 27 years.

I always used to look after the little queen and her attendants. I used to dress them up in their nice dresses, do their hair for them, make their faces up for them. Then we went to a meeting one night, along Christchurch Street at the Council offices, and Mr Cornish [President of Frome Carnival] said, 'Has anyone here got any idea what we can have for Carnival, for a change?'. I said, 'Yes, I have. What about having a Grandma Queen?'.

We used to do the lorry, my husband and I. One year we had three great big swans my husband made. He was a builder and decorator, he was very, very clever, he was. He made these beautiful swans, and at the back of the lorry he painted a castle with a path coming down and the little queen and her attendants were in a carriage pulled by these swans. And each swan had a teddy bear on them. I used to love doing the lorry. It was hard work but it was lovely.

Daisy Bane

Beswick's women in their 1948 Robin Hood entry

Wallbridge Mills' 1930 entry

Houston's Cloth Mill 1929 entry

Singer's Carnival Float, 'King Arthur and his Rusty Knights', c. 1970

Evelyn and Gerald in their courting days

Would Gerald and Evelyn Franks have met if it hadn't been for Frome Cheese Show and Frome Carnival? We shall never know.

[Evelyn] I was an evacuee in 1939, and I went to Draycott. In 1941 my parents were killed in the London Blitz and there was eight of us children in an evacuee house, and we all scattered round in different homes and that with foster people. Then in 1949 I came to Frome and was a nurse, started nursing. I met my husband – about a year later, wasn't it? 1950.

[Gerald] Cheese Show day used to be on the Wednesday of carnival week, and I was on duty for St John Ambulance at the Cheese Show Field, when we got a call for a gentleman who had a burst hernia. So we took him in an ambulance up to the Frome Hospital. And I met Evelyn up there, and we started talking, and one thing and another, and we made a date to meet on carnival night. She was on the nurses' float, and then we went to the fair afterwards. And then …

[Evelyn] I won the teddy, that's right. And of course we had to be back at the Nurses' Home by 10 o'clock, otherwise you got into trouble, and we went out on dates after that. Then we got married about two years later in 1954. I thought he was wonderful then, and we've been married 58 years.

Gerald and Evelyn Franks

An Exercise of Love and Care

Frome Victoria Hospital

WORKING WITH PEOPLE

This section brings together interviews with people working in health, schools, libraries and care settings. They all have in common that they work with people, rather than producing or selling a product. Many were brought to Frome by their work, rather than having grown up in the area.

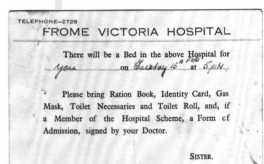

THE DISTRICT NURSES

Jean Gill moved to Frome in 1959 with her husband, Derek Gill, teacher and local historian.

I had tried to find work in Frome in Victoria Hospital, but they had no vacancies. But I managed to get a part-time district nursing job. Because I could drive I was given the use of a county car.

One patient I remember in particular, poor man, had pneumoconiosis from working in the mines. He was very ill. His very kind wife discovered that I was affected by morning sickness which wasn't helped by driving! She insisted that I didn't strain myself lifting her husband at all. I had some really lovely patients, one old lady, for some reason they had told her that she wasn't to get up and she certainly wasn't to use her sewing-machine, and she liked sewing. I didn't know that she'd been banned from using the sewing-machine so she got me to thread it for her because she couldn't see to thread it! Just one incident that sticks in my mind.
Jean Gill

Jean Gill

99

Frome Medical Practice

Frome Medical Practice staff in 2010, enjoying a social gathering. The photograph was taken outside the Rook Lane Chapel

Jude Curtis explained that district nurses are employed by the Primary Care Trust, but that these days they take more decisions.

My job is going out to people in their homes, keeping people in their homes of all ages not just the elderly. The sort of patients who now stay at home, many of whom, many years ago, would have automatically gone into hospital or into some form of residential care.

When I came here 20 years ago I was the youngest member of the team and now I'm almost the oldest and all the doctors are looking so much younger! We take a lot more decisions and the relationship that we have established here with the GPs is really very good indeed. We feel very strongly that we are part of the team and of course the patients benefit from that.

There are some real characters in Frome! It doesn't matter which area in Frome I might be, or perhaps in the villages, you cannot actually know what you are going to find the other side of the door. One of the things that I've really admired here is that there's a lot of close looking after of the different generations, turning to each other and looking after

each other and some really good care from neighbours, how much they get involved with looking after people who need help so that's really impressed me. **Jude Curtis**

Kate Greenwood

Kate Greenwood had worked in hospitals before moving to Frome in 1978.

When you are out there with a patient in their own home, they have got a different sort of status from when they are in hospital. When patients get into a hospital bed they seem to think, 'I'm in hospital, I'll do what I'm told', usually, whereas when they are in their own home they may think, 'Wait a moment, I think I don't want to do that. I don't want to get into bed'. You have to try and use your skills to get them to do what's best for them in their own home.

New Frome Community Hospital opened in 2008

A patient I went to in Frome for several years every day had a dog and a budgie. I remember once on Christmas day, my husband took the dog for a walk and then he cleaned the budgie out for her. He used to come round every Christmas Day and he has always done that and I would say that my husband was in the car and they would say, 'Oh bring him in'.

Kate Greenwood

Victoria Hospital Operating Theatre in the 1940s

Dr Bob Griffiths

Dr Mary Harrison

THE DOCTORS

Former GP Bob Griffiths, now retired, started work in Frome soon after Frome Medical Practice was set up at Park Road.

There were two medical practices in Frome, Rook Lane and the other West Lodge, each had four people, all men in those days. Then in 1969 they established the Health Centre in Park Road, the first Health Centre in Somerset. It was quite unique in Frome to have this virtually on the same campus as the Frome Victoria Hospital which was a community hospital. So it was the start of an integrated primary and secondary care service.

In 1971 the previous partner Dr David Joy, who had been in practice in Frome for 36 years, retired and they were looking for a new partner with an interest in anaesthetics. I had done a year's anaesthetics in Bath so I fitted the bill really. The previous year I had been doing anaesthetics, all my patients were fast asleep and then I arrived in Frome and they were all very talkative!

Bob Griffiths

Mary Harrison trained as a nurse then as a doctor at St Thomas' Hospital. She became the first woman GP at Frome Medical Practice.

I had always wanted to do medicine but my school didn't think I was going to be capable of it, so I went into the Nightingale Training School at Thomas' to do nursing. It was while I was a charge nurse that I had an amazing opportunity to change over to the medical school. At that time Thomas' had a very enlightened policy because they realised that a lot of people had had their careers messed up by the war. They decided it was quite a good idea to have an older element amongst their students, so they kept 20 places a year for older people. We had to do a year's preliminary science course to bring us up to date.

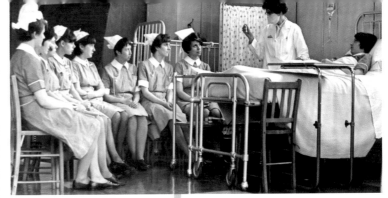

She joined Frome Medical Practice in 1975 as a trainee GP, just as Frome was expanding.

There were eight male partners. I was the first woman partner. For me it was quite exciting because the big estate of new houses down at Princess Anne Road [the Stonebridge estate] had just been built and therefore there were a lot of pregnant women and young families, so there was considerable opportunity. Several women liked to be looked after during pregnancy by a woman. At that time the majority of our deliveries took place in the Frome Victoria Hospital and I enjoyed being able to see somebody right through their pregnancy and then to watch the children grow up. One of the nicest things that people said to me when I retired was, 'We're not just losing a doctor, we're losing a friend'.

Mary Harrison

Student nurses in the 1960s

Jackie Lobley mid-80s above, and 1966 below

THE MIDWIFE

Jackie Lobley trained as a nurse in Bristol. She came to work at the newly opened Frome Health Centre as a practice nurse. Later she retrained as a midwife in Bath, and worked as a community midwife from 1980 to 2005, based in Frome Medical Practice and Frome Victoria Hospital.

We did do a lot of home deliveries. When the nation's home delivery rate was 1-2%, Frome Victoria was up to 11%. After 1945 it was considered not safe to have your baby at home. So medicine took over midwifery and therefore you didn't have your home deliveries. Later in the century, midwives were of the opinion that mothers actually did much better in a friendly home environment, that in fact home was not an unsafe place to deliver, provided that everything was normal within the pregnancy and there were no risk factors.

I think the births that go right, you don't remember those so much, but it's just an absolutely fabulous feeling after a delivery of having this new-born baby there and everything normal and seeing the mother breast-feed straightaway. A very memorable birth was in a bender across two fields off the A36 here locally. That was quite an ordeal. We had to be aware of 'What if there was an emergency?', so we had balloons tied on the gates, so that they knew where to go across the fields. Absolutely perfect.

I remember a water birth at home, I remember having to dive in deeper than I had planned! Having got wet through right to the waist and travelling home in the middle of the night, having taken wet clothes off. I just kept on hoping I didn't get stopped by the police.

Jackie Lobley

Jackie Lobley

THE HEALTH-CARE ASSISTANT

Gloria Wingrove was one of the workers made redundant when Beswick's closed in 2001. She has done various jobs in her life, and also completed an Open University degree, but this is the job she liked the best.

They put us all through interview training, so we knew what to expect, because most of us had been there so long it was something we had never ever experienced. I just applied for three different jobs because I was thinking reception-type work at the time. Two were at the doctors' practice but both jobs had already been taken and I ended up going to Social Services in Christchurch Street West. Frome Medical Practice contacted me after about six months of social services saying another position arose, 'Would I like to go up there?'. I joined as a receptionist

www.fromemedicalpractice.co.uk

and then I was asked, 'Would I be interested in doing health-care work?', and ended up as a health-care assistant. I hadn't thought about ever doing that job, but I've loved it.

Even working in a shop you don't really get to know people, whereas dealing with patients, especially if they're regular, it's like your friends all the time. I really like people and you couldn't wish for a better job than members of the public coming in to see you every 10 minutes.

Gloria Wingrove

Blanche Farley

THE DIRECTOR OF NURSING

Blanche Farley left school in 1952. After completing a secretarial course she trained in psychiatric and general nursing and worked for the Health Authority. She retired in 1991. She was Mayor of Frome in 2006/7, an honour she shares in this book with Russell Milne.

I came to Frome in 1987 to decommission the 52-bedded Selwood Hospital [one of three in Somerset for people with learning difficulties]. This was a joint project between the Health Authority and Somerset Social Services. Firstly, we tried to place the residents into suitable accommodation to meet their needs, ensuring that friends stayed together as far as possible. Secondly to ensure that staff, many of whom had worked there for years and were anxious about their futures, were properly advised.

Selwood Hospital, once Frome Workhouse, is now Ecos Court houses and flats (above). Map below.

A working party of staff and social workers advised on the residents' needs and groupings. I concentrated on the needs of the staff. We closed the hospital in six months. To the authorities it was a financial exercise but to me and my fellow workers it was an exercise of love and care.

Blanche Farley

THE PRACTICE MANAGER

Sue Palmer, among others, sought work when Selwood Hospital closed.

Sue Palmer

When my three children were a little bit older, I worked in Selwood Hospital as a nursing assistant, working nights so that in the daytime I was home for the children. I really loved it. I applied for a job working with social services in what was called the Core House on Somerset Road. There were about six or seven people from Selwood Hospital who moved in with staff and the intention was that they would be trained to be able to manage to live in the community. Then a job for a receptionist came up with the Frome Medical Practice, just round the corner, about 22 years ago. I applied and I got the job and I have stayed here ever since. I have had various different positions throughout the practice. When I first started we had one computer.   ***Sue Palmer***

THE VOLUNTEER

Muriel Chapman did a lot of voluntary work – with evacuees during the war, for Dr Barnardo's, WRVS, and the OXFAM shop. She worked as a volunteer at the health clinic in Cork Street, and much later at Park Road.

I did 25 years there. I was only a helper, just doing weighing or filing or whatever. We used to sell formula milk, all the things that babies needed, and we never used to see a man around the place. But by the time I had retired, they were coming in. I saw the children growing up and sometimes I used to get people say, 'I got the card you sent when my son or daughter was christened'. But not now because a lot of them are gone and it was the parents I knew rather more than the children. I did about 60 years of voluntary work but I enjoyed every moment and never regretted it. I think I was much better off, I know.

Muriel Chapman

THE TEACHERS

Eunice Overend was a rather special teacher.

Eunice Overend

On first finishing training I did supply teaching. I quite liked it in one sense because you could do what you liked. If they didn't know you and they played you up, you could arrive with a snake around your neck. I'd keep a grass snake, I knew where they lay and I'd fetch them when cool. If I had a class that didn't take much notice, I'd have one up my sleeve – you can't do it too often – and they'd pay attention! You wouldn't try an adder! In my classes I always had something different we could do, and if somebody brought along something I could change my lesson, I could change anything.

Eunice Overend

Eunice Overend's influence extended through a whole generation of Frome youth, as Paul Truscott, a carpenter, a member of the Frome Society for Local Study and a volunteer at Frome Museum, remembers.

Paul Truscott

I knew Eunice Overend from years back. We used to go down and visit her, like a lot of schoolchildren did, when she lived at Feltham Lane. I was doing little bits of work for her down there for her badgers. We built a badger run for her down there. She started talking about local history. I somehow found that fascinating and she was talking about the Frome Society, and she got me to join. There were a few youngsters back in the early days. And I got involved with that, going around some of the local factories which was what they did at the start. We visited practically all the factories when there were still factories in the town. They were just starting the museum down at Church Steps [now at North Parade] and I went down there and was helping painting and doing some of the carpentry work down there and I made a stand for the Singer's bell.

Paul Truscott

Frome Museum

The old building was replaced by a new building in 1977, then closed in 1989. Drawing by Isabel George

Margaret Binney

Isabel George taught art and pottery at Frome School of Art in Park Road, where she had been a student in the 1930s. She retired in 1982.

The first five years until Will went to school, I didn't work. Then they asked me if I would go back, and I did. And I actually stayed teaching art and pottery for quite a while. I went on working because I was involved with the leisure and pleasure classes, organising in the villages and villages halls. If people asked for a class, I would find a tutor for things like upholstery, art, sewing, dressmaking, things like that. It was very much a full-time job, and you had to go round and collect the money in the evenings. Quite a number of evening classes, especially the language classes, were held at the Grammar School, which is now Frome College. And in the village schools – we had a keep fit class going in the club-room of the pub in Beckington. It was a very interesting job.   **Isabel George**

Margaret Binney worked in schools and community education in Frome.

We were only going to stay here six months and here I am still! When we moved down I had the two girls and then I had Jonathan shortly after we moved here. I became a relief foster parent and round about that time as well I became involved with Community Education in Frome and I started to do quite a bit of training as a family learning tutor. So that was getting families together as a unit and learning together. The only thing that's left is Sure Start at the Key Centre and Hayesdown Children's Centre. Much of the family learning went completely.

I was going into schools where they specifically targeted groups of families and children. And that [work] was things like reading and writing with your child, simple sums with your child, cooking, family management, the whole circle of helping people with family life.   **Margaret Binney**

Sunday Schools were an important part of Frome life and churches provided a range of outings and clubs, as one teacher remembers.

I have lived in Frome since 1966 and my two children both went to Wesley School, which was a Methodist-based school. One of the teachers at the school was connected to Portway Methodist Church and she encouraged them to go to Sunday School. So as a result I went to see what was happening and got involved myself. We've been in contact ever since.

Performing the 'Loopy Loo' at the Frome Portway Chapel Sunday School Party

Both Church of England and non-conformist Sunday Schools held Bun Sunday processions at Whitsuntide. Banners were carried through the streets and at the end of the procession children would eat special, very large buns. Some of the banners survive in Frome Museum.

The Key Centre is a Children's and Healthy Living Centre providing a nursery and all year childcare, in partnership with Christ Church School, Somerset County Council and the Mount Community Association. Sarah Bullmore, headteacher and centre manager, discusses its success.

Bun Sunday 1940

M y vision for the school, right from taking on the headship, was to bring agencies in to support local families. A Children's Centre is a universal provision, so it's open to anybody. The trick is that you are able to identify people who are vulnerable. But who is to say when we are vulnerable? It's not necessarily about how healthy or wealthy you are. It's not about how clever you are. We can all be vulnerable at different times. The skill is then to bring into the centre those who would benefit from say a parenting session or some support with benefits or housing or writing a CV. It's about the needs of families and changes that happen

Sarah Bullmore

in your life. We work as a network of professionals. What I do see now with families is parents' confidence levels changing in terms of their own ability to be a parent. **Sarah Bullmore**

THE CARERS

The first two stories are about caring for children and families; the third is from Gerald Franks, a volunteer, about older people. For Elaine Pugsley, being a parent and volunteer led to social work.

Elaine Pugsley

When I moved to Frome I found out about the mother and toddler group at Christ Church Hall, run by the Health Centre – it was wonderful. I took Martin to the Opportunity Playgroup in Wesley Lower School. This was 1976. I went and helped there and Martin played with the other children. Next came the Toy Library – every parent and child could go and borrow an educational, stimulating toy for a period, and you also met other parents – it was somewhere you could go to chat. **Elaine Pugsley**

Anne Wallis came to Frome in 1968 with her family. She trained in social work and psychology and helped set up the first Family Centre in Frome.

Anne Wallis

Family Centres were mentioned in the Children Act which had just come out [1989] so I thought, 'What we're doing in social work is not enough. What we need to do is to help young parents, really young parents to raise children and not where everything's gone wrong, to help them before they go wrong'. National Children's Homes had got quite a big centre in Bristol so we spoke to them and they were interested. There were discussions between NCH, Somerset Social Services and the NHS and that's how it all got set up. It started in the old Wesley School and had a policy of being open to everyone. **Anne Wallis**

Frome Day Centre runs twice weekly at Frome Town Football Club [Badger Hill]. It began life in Gentle Street, closed in the 1990s and reopened in 2001 at the Assembly Rooms, with Gerald Franks' help.

I kept on at councillors to try and get another day centre and I couldn't get anywhere till I met Sue Klepper, who was on the council at the time. We started up in the Assembly Rooms. We provide a lunch for everybody, a two-course meal for £5. At the moment we're doing physical exercise in the morning on Mondays, sitting in chairs, the zumba once a month.

Then we have line dancing every Thursday afternoon. And that's open to anyone of 50 upwards, they don't have to come to lunch. I put in for any grant that's going to keep us going. We got a grant because a lot of older people want to learn about computers, we've got about 40 on our lists want to learn. Since we moved to the football club, we're getting 80-plus on a Monday, about 50-60 on a Thursday. We're getting a lot more than we were at the Assembly Rooms. There's plenty to do – it keeps me busy! I feel I'm doing something. **Gerald Franks**

Frome Day Centre

THE LIBRARIANS

Jane Evans, Mary Henderson and Wendy Miller-Williams have given between them 50 years of library service in Frome.

Jane Evans was born in 1948 and attended Oakfield School. After a spell at Butler and Tanner she got the job she wanted.

Mr Richard Lewis was the English teacher and in charge of the library for Oakfield, and that's where I spent all my lunch hours and breaks. I used to go into the library and have my little enamel badge saying 'Librarian' and that's probably where I got the bug, I think!

Frome Library

The Old Library

Jane Evans

Wendy Miller-Williams

Mary Henderson

I went for an interview in [the library at] the Temperance Hall at the bottom of Catherine Street. But it had a concrete floor. They discovered a crack in it and they had to move out to the Baptist chapel school-room, further up. There was a little lobby where I used to leave my bike when I cycled in.

The library stayed there for 18 months while the octagonal building now occupied by Ellenbray's and often called The Old Library was built.

It had a flat roof which leaked. And the spiral staircase which is still there was just the bare wood with no hand-rail. It was quite dangerous so they had to put a rail in and put some rubber treads on the steps. But after the other one, it was wonderful! **Jane Evans**

Wendy Miller-Williams arrived at Frome Library in 1987 and is still here. The opening of the present library in 1990 was a great event.

It was very exciting being involved in the new library build. We went away for days on end to library suppliers, choosing all these new books. Right from the start we would have occasional talks, we'd have speakers come, we'd have author talks. It was the Frome Festival that really kicked off the activity programme here. **Wendy Miller-Williams**

As Frome has grown, numbers have increased and what people expect of their library has changed. Mary Henderson explains:

Now we have the Council Information Point, we have the Tourist Board, we have various groups in – groups in from the Job Centre and young people that come along to update their CVs and apply for jobs using the computers. That's how we've gone from being a building that provides books and information to now being a community hub.

Mary Henderson

Jobs for the Taking

PLANTS AND ANIMALS

Lin Walton trained as a teacher and Brian Walton had worked in the food industry. They bought Cherry Tree Farm in Spring Gardens initially as a home for themselves and for Brian's mother.

[Lin] We had this lovely house, lots of outbuildings and an acre of land. Brian was fed up with his job, and we were watching this television programme called 'The Good Life' that followed a group of people who dropped out and chose alternative life-styles. And one of the couples had small children, they bought a goat farm in Wales, although they'd never kept animals or had any experience in the food industry. We were watching the man trying to mend a fence, and Brian said, 'For goodness sake, I could do that and I could make cheese', and that really set the seed of the goats. Brian's granddad had kept goats and I'd worked out that Brian was very good with animals and his father had been in farming, so I wasn't worried about the animal husbandry side.

[Brian] I thought about ice-cream because it has added value, and at the end of the day you have to turn a cheaper product into a more expensive one to make a profit. Early on we would only have small quantities, so we looked at doing local shops and at the time the Farmers' Markets arena was building up. We found a lot of small local customers to sell to.

[Lin] We always had an open farm policy. If anybody turned up we'd always say, 'Oh, d'you want to go and see the goats?'. I'd be bottle-feeding, Brian'd be milking. We wanted it to be a community farm, in the sense people would feel welcome there.

[Brian] In the meantime, a lot of the supermarket chains were recognising a demand for high quality local food. Eventually we ended up supplying

Lin and Brian Walton sell Cherry Tree Farm products at Corsley Show in 2000

Cherry Tree Farm's logo

the local stores of Safeway and Somerfield with our produce. Once we'd gone through the Head Office approval, we had carte blanche to go to a store manager. **Lin and Brian Walton**

This strategy eventually led to disaster with a marketing company letting them down in discussions with Sainsbury's, their own discussions with Tesco grinding to a halt, and foot-and-mouth cutting local sales. Cherry Tree Farm and the goats had to be sold.

Keith Higgins wavered between his interest in animals and the open-air life, and the good money that he could earn at Express Dairies at Oldford.

I wanted to do a job with animals and the nearest thing I could do at the time was to work on a farm, and there was a job vacant down at Hill Close Farm, Spring Gardens, which belonged to Mr Herbert Carey. I had one Saturday afternoon off every three weeks. I worked there two years.

Then when his son Philip left college there was not enough work for us all to do. I went down to work at Express Dairies at Oldford and it was quite an experience being indoors all the time after being with the animals and things. It was a bit different but I did like it.

The creamery at Oldford has had various owners and names over the years but is still operating

Later, Philip Carey took on Dairy House Farm, Beckington, a much bigger farm, and he asked me if I would like to work for him, which I did. After two years I returned to the factory because the money almost trebled compared with farm work. Three weeks' paid holiday which was very good, your free milk and a lot of dairy products at lower prices.

It was lovely down there, friendly and very quiet with the River Frome flowing along in front of the factory. When more buildings were put up it was diverted away from it. When I first went there we were so easy-going and together, but the larger the workforce became, with many workers coming from our other factories in London, the more you became a number rather than an individual. At the end of my time there they began to cut back again on staff. I worked there for 26 years and then I was made redundant. **Keith Higgins**

Nursery gardening was also important in the Frome area. Jeff Smith was keen on growing plants from age six or seven.

I can remember as a youngster, my father giving me my first packet of seed, which was French Marigolds. He gave me a half tray, got me to put some compost in it, level it off and firm it down. I'd pick out the seed from the packet and place it around the tray, then a little sieve, lightly cover and water it and do a little label. Then I'd have a surprise, probably about 10 days or so later, them starting to come up and getting excited because I thought the whole packet had come up and I wanted to prick out every single one, which I did, into little pots and grow them on and then going off and selling them for something like three pence.

Jeff Smith

Jeff worked at several nurseries before setting up on his own, which lasted from the mid-1980s till the mid-1990s. It was a precarious way of earning a living – an overdraft every winter, paid back the next summer.

Well, Mother was getting older, she was doing less which is understandable and I couldn't be in two places at once. I couldn't be out selling and also back doing work as well. I don't know, we just sort of sat down one day and thought, 'What are we doing?'. We were making a living but just about. So we just made the decision, you know, one of those decisions in life that you have to, and looking back at it now I'm not sorry, because the retail plant trade has changed a hell of a lot with the competition of supermarkets. So I'm not sorry to come out of it. **Jeff Smith**

Lamb Brewery workers

BREWING

One man recalls his father's work for two of Frome's breweries. The Lamb Brewery was originally situated in the triangle between Christchurch Street East, Gorehedge and Keyford Street, later acquiring premises on the north of Christchurch Street East, including the former malthouse, which is now apartments. The United Brewery lay to the south-east of Horton Street on land now covered by houses.

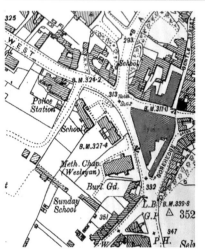

Marked in brown on 1903 maps, the Lamb Brewery, above, and United Brewery, inset right

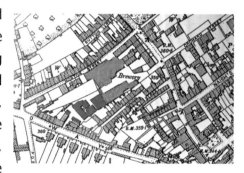

M y father worked for the United Brewery and the Lamb Brewery. He used to go out on the lorries, delivering beer you see, from Frome United Brewery. That was in the late 1940s, 50s. He used to take me with him in the lorry, on my school holidays and that. We used to go all round the pubs of the district, delivering beer. It was all wooden casks then, all the old wooden barrels then, you see. There were no metal casks then.

Trevor Biggs was born in 1939, and got an apprenticeship at Wilson and Scotchman in Keyford, now the site of the Cooperage houses. Wilson and Scotchman had begun making wooden vats, and this side of the business was still in place, especially for cider-making.

Below, The Lamb Brewery

W ilson and Scotchman's were a brewery engineering company. The department that I went into was the coppersmith's. At that time all the main plant were made of copper. The job involved going out on site quite a bit, and I think after only about a month I went over to Usher's in Trowbridge. That was my first introduction to a brewery. Although I lived next door to the United Brewery, I'd not been inside one. I travelled all over the place and I was there for 18 years.

Trevor describes the eventful transportation of a boiling copper from Frome to Wetherhead's Brewery, Marlow.

It was built in the yard at Keyford, and when it was finished it was lifted up on a lorry. The copper was 17 foot across. Reading was the only town on the route to Marlow and the police had to be notified. The lorry picked up a police escort outside Reading and the police took them through Reading, up an avenue of trees, and he had to weave in and out. We were up there when the boiling copper arrived, you see, and it came into the yard with all the branches of the trees, and the twigs and all the leaves sticking out. And they parked up in the yard and Sparrows Cranes of Bath, who had the biggest crane in Europe at the time, called Lorraine, they were there.

Above, the boiling copper made by Wilson and Scotchman loaded onto a lorry for delivery to Marlow

They slung it right up over the buildings, and there was a guy on the top of the roof just signalling to the chap on the crane, and he brought it over and he dropped it through the roof absolutely spot on. The boiling copper was 17 foot, and they had an 18 foot hole. He dropped that down through and they just positioned it – the guy stopped him at a foot before it got to where it had to stand, and just turned it to where it had to go, and he signalled and let that down absolutely perfect. I was there, I was in charge of the job. **Trevor Biggs**

Construction of a copper under way in Wilson and Scotchman's yard

© Mendip District Council

The former feather factory, Willow Vale, above, before, and below, after conversion into flats

© Mendip District Council

BUILDING TRADES

Paul Truscott trained as a carpenter and worked for his uncle, appropriately enough called David Carpenter, who lived in Weymouth Road opposite the park gates.

He was a carpenter, as were most of his sons, when they all left school and came to work for him. I didn't go to college at all, I just learned everything from him. I worked for him for nearly 20 years until he died. My aunty carried on the firm for another year, then myself and his younger son carried on working together. I was self-employed then, until Damian Kelly (D.J. Kelly Ltd) wanted some carpenters, and I was with him until I retired Christmas 2010. Most of our work was in Frome. We did the conversion of the old feather factory in Willow Vale into flats. It was completely derelict when we moved in there. I've always preferred fiddly jobs.

Paul prefers traditional craft work, such as box-frame sash windows and staircases; he dislikes modern materials such as MDF and the use of pre-fabricated roof frames and windows. The feather factory conversion was a good example of contemporary use of traditional methods.

I always enjoyed roofing, particularly cut roofs. Anybody can put a truss roof on – you just want a hammer and nails. A cut roof is when you just have a pile of timber and you gotta measure it, cut it, cut all the joints and fit it with hips, valleys, dormers. It's proper roofing, rather than a truss roof that comes in manufactured and it's just stuck up on the walls. When I did the roof at Willow Vale, it all had to be done in green oak, there were massive great beams there and I had to splice a few of them in. Some of them would take me a couple of days just to put a new piece of timber in. I enjoyed that in there, once we cleared the pigeons out the way!

Paul Truscott

Ian Spearing did his carpentry training with Hodder's, on Broadway, one of Frome's largest building firms. They were also undertakers and wheelwrights.

I left school in 1948 at 15 and started work at Hodder's. I don't know how Mum got hold of the information but she wanted me apprenticed as a carpenter-joiner and Hodder's had the reputation of being the best builders in the town at the time. The first five years were my apprenticeship years and they expected you to give up two evenings of your week to go to the School of Art and Science in Park Road for building classes.

When I got to Hodder's we did undertaking and funeral directing so I was involved in some of that, making coffins and actually putting the bodies in them and being a pallbearer, which was good experience.

The apprentices used to go through some kind of initiation like sending you out for imaginary items. The foreman, Jack Crowther, sent me down to Rawling's, which was next to the Memorial Theatre, to get a stick of belt dressing and I would not go because I thought, 'These guys are sending me on a goose chase', and I didn't believe him. In the end I realised and I had to cycle all the way down to Rawling's and get this stick of belt dressing, which was genuine, and come back. Well that was a standing joke, but of course as years unfolded I had a couple of apprentices myself including Kalem Seconds. I did some terrible things to him by sending him off for board stretchers and things like this, but that's him right there in the photo on my bike that I used to ride to work on. **_Ian Spearing_**

Top, inside Hodder's carpenter's shop, 1957; middle, Kalem Seconds outside Hodder's wheelwright's shop; bottom, Hodder's employees as funeral directors in the works' yard

Premises of Hodder and Sons, which was opposite the Ring o' Bells pub on Broadway

A third carpenter, Robert Hawker, worked for many different firms in the town. Robert went on day release to Frome College in Park Road to get his City and Guilds qualification in carpentry. National Service was like a continuation of his civilian job.

I left school at 14 in 1945 and worked in a paper shop down Cheap Street called Ward's. Then I went as apprentice carpenter to the builder's, Hodder's, in Broadway. I worked there till I went to National Service when I was 19.

After basic training, I went into the Royal Engineers to the railway camp at Longmoor, Hampshire, and that's where I stayed. I was a signalman for a while, then a carpenter, so I didn't move far from Frome actually! I came back to Hodder's for a while, then after that I had so many jobs, too many to remember really. You just went round different places and asked. Jobs was easier to get then than now. I worked for loads of firms: Carroll's, Mildav and Mordel's of Frome, Maslin's of Devizes, Dell's of Trowbridge. You did then.

Robert Hawker

Ray Trowbridge

Ray Trowbridge completed a five-year apprenticeship at Parsons of Westbury. It included a lot of college study to obtain his City and Guilds certificate. He worked for a time in the maintenance department at Wallington Weston but then branched out on his own.

I was very friendly with a plumber, Reg Davies, of Hodder's, the builders, which was down the bottom end of Broadway. He got in contact with a builder, Colin Loveridge, and he came round to see me and said, 'Do you want a job?' He said he could either employ me or I could be self-employed. And I thought, 'Right, I've had enough of being employed', so I went self-employed and we worked together over 30 years nearly. And we had a very good relationship. He was a plasterer by trade, but I ended up by doing plaster, plumbing, bricklaying – you name it, I done it. And for me it was good. If you vary your jobs it's a lot better. We used to do a lot of private work and then we got onto the Somerset County Council list to do maintenance in schools and various properties and we done every school in Frome. We stopped doing the county work because we were getting older and then I retired, or nearly. I still do some work. We did have a workshop in Castle Street that used to be an old mill or grain store. Up on the first floor was my workshop and an old hoist. It's houses now.

Above, the three-storey former mill or grain store on Castle Street, now a house, where Ray Trowbridge had his workshop

Ray Trowbridge joined the St John Ambulance Cadets as a boy. As an adult he held various posts of responsibility including divisional superintendent, and was a stalwart of the service.

Bill Ellis, who used to live next door to us in Lansdown Place, he was a driver. He'd have the ambulance parked outside his house on Sundays. One of our main things when I was driving the ambulance was maternity runs. I never had to be a midwife but one of my colleagues acted as midwife – we were only in our young twenties – and he delivered twins!

Ray Trowbridge

Inset left, Ray Trowbridge, second left, in the Frome St John Ambulance Cadets

TRANSPORT

Ron White was an enterprising Frome taxi-driver.

When I came out the army in 1954, my sister and her husband ran the Lamb and Fountain. I used to live there with them. Me being a young ambitious man, I acquired three taxis which I used to run from the Lamb and Fountain, and they were called the Fountain Taxi Service. And I was the first person in Frome that went to the Council offices and asked up there why it was we had no taxi ranks in Frome. And so he got this big old dusty book down off the shelf to look at all the old by-laws. And he said, 'Well, according to the by-laws of Frome, wherever there's a horse drinking trough, Mr White, you can apply for hire'. Now no-one had ever done this in Frome before. They'd all been what they call private hire, where you rang the yard and they sent a car out. So I had some signs made to put in the windscreen – 'Taxi for Hire' – and I was the first person in Frome to stand with a car with 'Taxi for Hire' on, because you weren't allowed to do that if you were private hire.   **Ron White**

The horse drinking troughs had related to the older horse-drawn Hackney carriages. Ron's presence by the Market Cross opposite the George created Frome's own 'taxi war' but eventually other taxi firms realised he was behaving perfectly legally, and followed suit. After 18 months, Ron gave up his taxi firm and went to Hertfordshire to work in the motor-racing industry with the likes of Colin Chapman and Stirling Moss.

Rodney Clarke drove first for Express Dairies, and later for English China Clay at Holwell Quarry.

I used to go down to South Wales on the Aust ferry boats with a 30cwt van, before the Severn Bridge was built. Sometimes that used to get very rough out in the Severn, and they'd go round in

The Lamb and Fountain, from which Ron White ran Fountain Taxi Service

Express Dairies' Wallbridge site in 1967, shortly before demolition

circles, deciding whether to go on or to go back. It used to be so rough that when they tried to dock, sometimes the dock'd be up there, the next moment it would be down there. And one of the chaps on the ferry would say, 'Right, when I say go, you go'. But no, we had some very hairy moments on that. There were three of them: the Severn King, the Severn Queen and the Severn Princess.

I left there in 1968 and went to work for English China Clay, driving a lorry, as a temporary measure, until something better come along. But then again, my wages doubled from one job to the other. If we were on 50 hours a week, we thought we were on short time. Especially come March when the councils used to spend all their money. We'd be night and day nearly – because the restrictions weren't quite as strict as they are now, driving lorries. So that was till something better come along. Thirty-eight years later I retired from there. We had a new General Manager come in one day and one of the girls said, 'This is Rodney. If we don't know what to do, we ask him'. Because I was the one there with the knowledge.

Rodney Clarke

Gerald Quartley on duty in the Rodden Road signal-box

Gerald Quartley has had a varied and full life, but remembers especially the years from 1979-84 when he worked at the Rodden Road signal-box where the Frome-Radstock railway left the main line. He is a mine of information about Frome, its people, industries and history.

The signal-box, if you're going out of Frome along Rodden Road, was on your left, on top of the bank, right beside the bridge. So it wasn't lonely in one respect because you could always look

Gerald Quartley in the Frome North signal-box, also seen below; bottom, Frome railway station

out the window or go out on the porch if there was no trains around, and watch the passers-by. We worked a three-shift system. The night shift was to cover the mineral traffic from Whatley quarry. During the day on the morning or afternoon shift you'd probably have a train crew come down from Westbury, and they might have to wait in a siding for a train to come back from the quarry. So they would come up in the signal-box and sit down and very often have a cup of tea.

The management were quite happy for you to listen to the radio, and you were quite at liberty to read a book if you wished. In the summer, if there was a cricket commentary, I listened to that. I didn't read many novels, probably history. I do like my books. And of course you had a cooker there, a Baby Belling, to cook a meal, because once you were there, you had to stop there! The farthest you could go would be to the outside toilet. But if you timed it right you could always nip up round the shops in St John's Road.

I had various, what my colleague used to term, extra-curricular activities. I had a thriving business chopping up kindling wood. I used to buy the scrap sleepers, the ones that were sub-standard, and I had a friend who had a truck, and I'd buy them and he would convey them up here for me and then I had several outlets in shops. I'd chop this wood and bundle it up. You'd see the chappie in charge of the track, the permanent way supervisor, and you'd say, 'Let me know if you've got anything about, Trevor'. 'Yes, OK.' So he'd make sure the sleepers were put somewhere handy, near the road, where you could pick them up. You could buy a damned great pile for a fiver.

Gerald Quartley

THE POST

David Barnes

David Barnes started work as a telegram boy at Frome Post Office, a rather military establishment in a 'tiny little sorting office' behind where Superdrug now is in the Market Place. It was 1951 and he was aged 15. He spent his whole working life there, except for National Service, which he spent in the Royal Engineers' Postal Service!

I went into the counter and said, 'I've come down about a job'. I was taken up to the Head Postmaster in his office and he asked me a few questions. I think I can remember him saying to me, 'Why would you want to come to the Post Office, Mr Barnes?'. And I said, 'I want to get on!'. And he seemed to be delighted with that. He took me into another office and I did an exam, you know, a common sense exam, to make sure that I wasn't a complete idiot. And he said, 'Right', and gave me a day to start. Amazing.

It was a dark blue, thick serge, uniform. They were very particular on you wearing a shirt, tie and clean shoes. The person in charge of the messenger boys inspected every day because you were going out to meet the public, you see, with the telegrams. People can't imagine now that hardly anyone had telephones, for years, and the only communication if someone had died or a baby was born was through a telegram. We were busy all day. You could have a telegram for Witham Friary and you'd be gone an hour, getting out there and getting back on the bike!

One of the things I liked about being a postman, you started at half-past four and you were out on the road by a quarter to seven, you were your own boss then for about three or four hours. It was lovely, you know, walking around the town. We had a social club, used to have a wonderful dinner dance every Christmas. All the children went to a Christmas party with a lovely spread of food and presents. All that is gone now, people got no time to run those things now. **David Barnes**

Frome Post Office in the Market Place

Trevor Weston also worked at Frome Post Office, but mostly delivered in Witham Friary. Leaving school in 1959, he found it easy to get a job.

I could have had five jobs in a week. Not great jobs because I wasn't brainy. I went down Moore's, the corn people, they've got the shop along Christchurch Street West. They had a mill down Wallbridge, and that's where I used to work. Mr Moore said, 'This isn't no job for you, no life for you. I'll talk to Mr Dean the postmaster. There's a vacancy if you want me to put your name forward'. So that's where I went, down the Post Office. I was happy down there, I loved it. I'd have worked for nothing in those days. Forty years delivering – I done mostly Witham Friary. I done that for, oh, 30 years. When I started it was all farm labourers, council workers, railway workers, and when I left it was all business people. But that's not just that village, it's every village.

Frome Post Office sorting office staff at Christmas 1967. The sorting office moved to its present site in Robin's Lane in 1990

I always used to say, 'If they just put somebody's name on there I could deliver it!'. Very strict, Mr Dean was, very strict. I remember one day I came in, and he said – we always used to call him Mr Dean or Sir, never Stan – he looked at me and said, 'Shoes, Mr Weston'. I knew what he meant, I had to clean my shoes. Nothing else was said. Next morning he come in, they were all buffed up.

I was on strike for nine weeks in 1971. It was about pay, but after that, we always had good pay rises. We were very poorly paid then. They offered us 8%, we wouldn't accept it. They offered us 9% and we accepted it. I don't know why! But I was lucky, I was out on the farms working, you know, they'd always give you cash in hand in those days. I used to say, 'Got any jobs going?'. 'Yes, come on out, I can have a day off.' We had some good fun there.

Trevor Weston

All Change

WARTIME

It must be obvious to the reader who has reached this point in the book that Frome has changed. For the better? For the worse? That is up to you to decide.

Looking back with a rather longer perspective, some of the greatest changes in the twentieth century came from outside, especially as a result of the two World Wars. The 1914-18 war is beyond living memory now, though still a part of family memories and stories. Within living memory, the war years of 1939-45 provide the background to many of the experiences and changes recorded in this book.

Diana Crossman is one person with vivid memories of being at school during the war, first at St John's Infants and then at Christ Church.

Diana Crossman, aged 6, in 1937, at St John's Infant School

We walked from Willow Vale through the Market Place, then up Cheap Street, then up the steps, and usually we walked up Gentle Street, which I think is the oldest street in Frome. At the top we turned left and we were there – at St John's School. We did this every morning until I was seven and then I went to Christ Church and war began. One of the chief memories of wartime, apart from carrying my gas mask every day, was that every time an air-raid siren went, we went into the church and we lay under the pews and the teachers would come and give us books to keep us quiet.

Diana Crossman

A number of Frome firms were involved in the war effort. Nott's Industries, as any visitor to Frome Museum will discover, was the largest manufacturer in the United Kingdom of 'Carley' life rafts. These featured memorably in the 1942 war film, 'In Which We Serve' which centres around a group of survivors clinging to a Carley life raft. Singer's was making armaments.

The 'Works Wonders' concert, in which all performers were from the factory, was filmed in one of the Adderwell Works buildings and went out 'live', described as 'a lunch-time concert presented to their fellow workers by members of the staff of a large munitions work somewhere in England'.

Houston's was used as a store by the Bristol Aeroplane Company, and never went back to cloth production.

Most notably, the Portsmouth firm of G.E. Evans [Evans Engineering] was evacuated to Frome and occupied the Adderwell Works of Butler and Tanner. This brought new people into the town, but also led to change of occupation for some residents. Marjorie Holly, née Bratten, went to Evans in 1942 at the age of 14 direct from Milk Street School. She worked in the wages office and says they employed about 800 workers at the peak of production, which included glider undercarriages and other aircraft components ready for the invasion of Europe in 1944/45. She wanted to go to Portsmouth in 1945 but her parents thought she was too young.

Evans was a high profile firm during the War, and visitors included Queen Mary and Sir Stafford Cripps, Minister of Aircraft Production. The BBC recorded several 'Workers' Playtime' concert parties there. Jack Evans, a cine-film enthusiast, recorded one of them for posterity. There was also boxing and Tom Upshall remembers that Jimmy Wilde, a famous Welsh boxer, 'the finest boxer we ever had', was guest of honour at a dinner following a boxing evening at the factory. He had been world flyweight champion in 1916.

While most of the firm went back to Portsmouth in 1945, the engine division remained in Frome, next to the old gas works site at Welshmill. For Michael Penny and his family, Frome became their home. Their Portsmouth house was destroyed in the war, his father stayed on in Frome, and then in 1956 when the engine division finally left Frome, he preferred to stay in the town, with five children, including Michael, settled at school.

Carol McGeorge's family made a similar decision. Her father, a strong union man, became a JP and governor of the Grammar School. He had been brought up in an orphanage and found in Frome the warm community he had missed as a child. Carol says, 'I was born in Frome in the old Victoria Hospital. I love Frome'.

Vivien Kenney's mother now lives at Rowden House but came to Frome from Portsmouth in 1940. Her father was a Frome boy and they married in 1945. There was some movement in the reverse direction too. Pam Parker has an aunt in Portsmouth who worked at Evans. She and her sister were Frome girls and both married Evans' men and went back to live in Portsmouth.

The final word on Evans goes to Mary Corbett. Her mother Charlotte Elliott and grandmother Maria Coleman were two Frome women drafted in to war work at Evans.

Above, women watch the 'Works Wonders' concert and guns are assembled at Evans Engineering's Adderwell Works

Below, a boxing event at the Adderwell Works

Workers at G.E. Evans [Evans Engineering] in Butler and Tanner's Adderwell Works

The photograph of workers at Evans Engineering includes my mother. She is the lady centre front in the floral apron. They were working on bomb containers I was told. My grandmother, Maria Coleman, worked in the packing department making packing boxes. **Mary Corbett**

Mavis Gray was working at Butler and Tanner at the time, and rather than being sent with other workers to the Selwood works or to Bath Press to continue printing, she was transferred to war work.

During the War we had to move back to the old Butler and Tanner building in Selwood Road. The factory at Adderwell Road was taken over by Evans, a firm evacuated from Portsmouth. I got sent on war work at Tool and Gauge, first of all where the laundry was in Vicarage Street.

But then that was too small, so later in Crown Yard, down the lane beside the Crown, behind the Post Office. We were working from 7am to 7pm, making tools for other factories. You had to learn to use micrometers. I was the only Frome girl there at first. Didn't they take it out on me! They thought I was a country bumpkin. **Mavis Gray**

Second World War bomb damage in Broadway

In fact the firm was an off-shoot of a Cheltenham aircraft manufacturer called Rotol, settled in Crown Yard, Frome, by the Ministry of Supply in 1940 and managed by Reggie West. His son is Michael West, the current Managing Director of Frome Tool and Gauge, established as an independent company in 1946. Its factory was in Cork Street, and in 1964 it moved to the Marston Trading Estate where it now employs 30-35 people.

The fact that so much war work was going on in Frome seems to have been kept a closely guarded secret. Only three bombs actually fell on Frome, but one of them killed an air-raid warden and another produced major devastation in Broadway on 12 April 1941. The blast was so great that windows of houses in Nunney Road were blown out. Frome and its inhabitants were shaken. Hilary Daniel recorded a talk for Frome FM about wartime in Frome.

On Good Friday 1941 a couple of sticks of bombs were dropped across Frome, one up at the Mount and one in what is now Queen's Road. The one in Queen's Road killed an air-raid warden, and a house in Broadway was blown up the next day by a bomb that had a delayed fuse on it. **Hilary Daniel**

Hilary Daniel

Reproduced by permission
of English Heritage

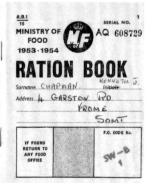

For some people, war work had its comical side, and Isabel George's 'war work' still makes her laugh today.

I had to give up the Art College, because I got drafted in connection with a catering firm, a rather upmarket confectioner's in the Market Place called Wickenden's. And they did a great deal of very posh catering and weddings and things and they were rather elderly and I went originally to cope with the ration coupons part of the business. As the war went on I gradually worked my way down, because, you know, staff left and got drafted into the army or the air force. And I stayed on, and finished doing the washing-up once at a wedding in the Masonic Hall, because the woman who usually did it just couldn't come that day, and they said, 'Would you?'. And I said, 'Yes, yes'. And I was so pleased because at the end of it the best man came out and gave me five shillings!

Isabel George

Ron White has more troubling memories of the War. He was six years old at the time.

This whole area in front of the new library, there was hundreds of soldiers that came back from Dunkirk with no shoes, boots, no shirts, terrible state, and all the women of Frome were giving them tea, putting blankets round them, and I've never, ever seen a photograph or anyone refer to that incident at all. My father used to drive for Roads Reconstruction during the war, and he went off for three or four weeks at least, maybe longer, transporting all these soldiers from Dunkirk from the coast inland. And they obviously brought a whole load to Frome. There must have been 200 sat down on the ground in front of the library. There was one chap sat on the floor with a blanket over him, and opposite, where the little footbridge is now, the ground used to come right down to river level there, and there was a young girl with a baby in a pram on the other bank watching what was going on. She must have let go of the pram and it careered down the bank and straight into the river, with the baby in it. And one of these chaps jumped up, threw his blanket off, and he dived in. There was a very high bank this side with all brambles and he dived right over the bushes into the water, took a hell of a chance because there were places where it was very shallow, and got this baby out. And he'd just come back from Dunkirk! **Ron White**

Frome Company Home Guard on parade along Christchurch Street West, inset left, and in the Market Place, above

One of the returners from Dunkirk married Winifred Fairhurst.

He was a regular in the Royal Artillery. When they came back from Dunkirk, some of them never had no boots on or anything. They were all dirty and wet. And they came through and we gave them cups of tea. Then they went somewhere else and got sorted out and then they came back to Frome. I met John at a dance in the Keyford Drill Hall and we got married in 1942. He was a Wigan boy.

Winifred Fairhurst

In the period leading up to the D-Day landings in Normandy, Frome was full of soldiers – British, Commonwealth and American. They were based at Longleat, Marston House and Orchardleigh. It was the American

133

Air Raid Wardens outside the Blue House in 1942

Frome Company Home Guard on parade

Frome Home Guard 'A' Company Band

soldiers who made the greatest impression, as a long-term resident of Trinity [or Chinatown, as the Americans called it] remembers.

During the war, see, the American GIs were based out at Marston House. They used to flock into Frome. They used to all congregate down Chinatown because of the pubs and the girls. I remember stories of them taking money off the Americans, and charging them the earth for their drink, watered-down drink with hardly any alcohol in it. The GIs didn't know what money they were giving them, they'd just hand them a handful of money and say, 'A pint of beer'. 'Got any gum, chum?' 'That's where it comes from, doesn't it?'

Jim White and Hilary Daniel also remember the gum-chewing Americans.

My earliest memory of Frome was seeing the railings being cut down outside Ames, Kent and Rathmore's offices in Bridge Street. It must have been about 1942 when things were quite grim. And my next memory is of just before D-Day getting gum thrown up to the top window above my dad's shop on The Bridge by black GIs. And I can remember standing there with no clothes on with my brother because it was very hot, in June. At that time I was three-and-a-half. And soldiers fighting in the Market Place and throwing huge thunderflashes around which they used to use in training. They sounded like shells going off. Usually Australians and New Zealanders were fighting and of course the place was full of American GIs as well. *Jim White*

Towards the middle of the War, the Americans arrived and there were vast numbers of them in various camps around the town. The Americans really made quite a difference to the town. Chewing gum was what we boys were most interested in, nylons were what the girls were most interested in.

Any American who appeared was surrounded by a gang of youngsters, all trying to listen to his wonderful way of talking and to see what goodies you could beg out of him. There were black soldiers and white soldiers there in those unreconstructed days. Unfortunately, considerable fights used to break out in the town centre between black and white soldiers and in the end an arrangement was made whereby whites were allowed in on one day and on alternate days the black soldiers were coming in. And my mother, who worked at the Women's Voluntary Service [WVS] canteen, said they were always very pleased on the 'black' nights because they were so much more polite and understanding than the white soldiers.

Hilary Daniel

The British restaurant occupied temporary premises in Cork Street car park for the last two years of the Second World War. It served meals, snacks and drinks to a wide variety of local people, especially workers at the factories near the town centre, and people who had run out of ration coupons! Run by Frome Urban District Council, it served an average of 2,500 dinners, teas and suppers per week.

EVACUEES

A surprising number of our interviewees took in evacuees or came to Frome as evacuees. It is not possible to include all their stories, but we offer a sample here. Caring for these evacuees was an important part of war work in the broadest sense. Ray Daniel is Hilary's brother.

My father died when I was three. I don't know whether I can remember him or whether it's people talking about him, but my mother brought us up. She was a very strong woman. She did both tasks of bringing us up, father and mother jobs. She worked during the War,

"UNION JACK" BRITISH RESTAURANT

•

JUNE 22nd, 1943

OFFICIAL OPENING

BY

COUNCILLOR H. M. SCOTT, J.P.
Chairman
Frome Urban District Council

SUPPORTED BY

COUNCILLOR F. MILTON RUSS, J.P.
Vice-Chairman

AND

MEMBERS OF THE COUNCIL

Menu.

Roast Beef, Churchill
Pudding, Yorkshire
———
Roast and Boiled Potatoes
Woolton
Spring Cabbage
Somerset
———
Cold Meat and Salad
Boiled Potatoes
———
Sultana Victory Roll
Custard Sauce
———
Blancmange Royal
———
Creamed Rice and Prunes
———
Biscuits and Cheese
———
Coffee

munitions work as part of the war effort. At that time our grandparents, who were living in Bath Street, both died and we moved into the house and we lived there until the end of the War. **Ray Daniel**

Their large house at Marston Gate was then used by some of the considerable numbers of evacuees, children and adults, who arrived in Frome in 1939 to 1940.

Ray Trowbridge had a similar experience.

There were quite a few families living in the house in Broadway, because it was the War – my parents, my mother's sister and her husband and family, my grandmother and grandfather, and two evacuees – a houseful. **Ray Trowbridge**

Both these photos were taken in Muriel Chapman's garden at 4 Garston Road: above, evacuees Beryl and Adrienne; below, Adrienne and Edwina

Muriel Chapman and her husband did not have children of their own, and Muriel has vivid memories of the evacuee children who stayed with them.

They looked poor little things there on the doorstep. They were named Joan and Violet Ogare. I thought I must give them a bath and when I stripped them, they were full of flea bites all over their bodies. And when I looked at their hair, they had lice. I had never seen lice before, I must confess, so I popped them in the bath and cut their hair. However, they were lovely children. They came in one day with an armful of red flowers and said, 'We brought you some flowers'. And I looked and it was bean flowers. I used to take them out to see the neighbours' children, if they had any little ones. So it was no trouble whatsoever.

Later, other children came to live with Muriel Chapman, and the families have maintained contact since.

Adrienne, her parents were killed in the Balham Tube Disaster on October the 14th 1940. So I had her right the way through until she was 16. Yes,

because she was going to a business course in Minehead but she used to come back for holidays or we used to go there. She's 83 now.

Edwina was a lovely girl. When I wasn't very well, she looked after my husband and made his breakfast. When she left, she went back to London and she married a Pole. I had one other, Beryl. She was very nice as well. I had her with Adrienne, and also a cat. They were all I had, but I had no trouble whatsoever with them, only the usual childhood things you know. But I couldn't say anything because I was full of life when I was their age.

Muriel Chapman

Zelda Brown

One of the most interesting pieces of evidence to come to light about evacuees in Frome consists of a pile of letters written by Zelda Brown to her parents back in London. She was a clever, precocious teenager who stayed with Mr and Mrs Lapham at 84, Nunney Road, and studied at Frome Grammar School as well as attending evening classes organised by the Workers' Educational Association [WEA]. Much later she became well known in London as Zelda Curtis, campaigner for the rights of older people. In these extracts, she reflects on wartime shortages, weather and social life in Frome.

Zelda Brown, second left, and some of her friends in Frome

Owing to the War, the school is short of paper and books, and I am not fully equipped with suchlike. Down here it's as bad as in Finland! We are absolutely frozen up in the house. No cold water, no hot water, no water in the lavatory! The other day we had a slight thaw and all the water came through the ceiling. Now it's frozen again, and we are expecting a burst. For water to wash ourselves in, we have to collect the snow and melt it. But still we keep smiling!

The Grand, one of Frome's cinemas of the time [now the Frome Memorial Theatre].

Wouldn't you think that in the country the boys and girls would be less grown-up than town children, who are supposed to have seen life? Well, they are not! Definitely! The girls and boys here are very grown-up in their outlook and their ways, and we're all very sensible in class, having lots of debates and arguments on various subjects. We all have fun together and we're carefree, but there's only one thing that I hate about Frome, and that is the gossip.

Do you know, if I go to the pictures with Mr and Mrs Lapham, they sometimes say to me, 'Look, see that person in the second row from the back, well he's not a Frome boy'. That shows you that people know everybody in Frome, and when I first came to Frome, within a week, everybody knew there was a stranger in Frome, and by the time I went to school, they all knew me as 'that London girl who's staying with the Laphams'.

Zelda Brown

POST-WAR

The changes and experiences of wartime, good and bad, influenced the course of events after the War. People had new and different expectations. Before the War, access to doctors and medicine had depended on money, and as we have recorded, most Frome families were not well off. The setting up of the National Health Service was one of the first and most important changes that came out of the Second World War. If Britain was to rebuild its economy, and continue to play a major role in the world, great improvements in schools were necessary and this is fully reflected in the experience of Frome families. Full employment, at least for a time, became an aim of government and the prosperity of Frome in the 1960s and 1970s was a reflection of this. Equally, guaranteed prices

© Mendip District Council

for farmers was a way of ensuring that Britain would be less dependent on imported food.

There was also concern about the dreadful housing conditions in the older parts of Frome, especially in Trinity. The demolition of the northern part of Trinity and its replacement by modern council housing in the 1960s was no doubt begun with the best of intentions. But the much-praised rebuilding and conservation of the area south of Trinity Street showed what might have been, as did the conversion of Selwood Print Works into flats.

The stories we have been lucky enough to hear and record tell of many changes. Large employers have gone out of business, under the pressure of national and global competition, as the control of our national government over the economy weakened in the 1980s and 1990s. Production has moved elsewhere, either within the UK [Wallington Weston and Cuprinol] or abroad [Beswick's]. The great survivors – the Victorian firms of Butler and Tanner and Singer's – are much smaller than they were in the past. Small nurseries have given way to garden centres, corner shops to supermarkets. Small farms have been gobbled up by big farms, and the market that served the farming community moved right out of Frome, even though it is still called 'Frome Market'. Even the Cheese Show has moved out of town and is now held on a Saturday, rather than on a Wednesday, at a site at West Woodlands.

Above left and centre, properties in Trinity ripe for demolition and during the demolition process; right, the award-winning Piggeries development

One of Frome's lost corner shops

The properties in Sun Street, below, are an example of how parts of Frome have been rescued and renovated

Before ...

... and after

There are still jobs in Frome, in the health service, schools, banks and building societies, and offices. There are important employers, some on the Marston Trading Estate and many of them quite recent, who are not represented in our book. Many people travel out of Frome to work in out-of-town supermarkets, or to Longleat or Center Parcs. Some go to Trowbridge, Bristol and Bath, or even London. An increasing number of people work from home or are part of the growing artistic and craft communities in Frome. A range of new housing is being constructed in the town. In the 1960s Frome's population was 10,000. By 2010 the population had grown to 25,000 and continues to rise.

What else has changed? Trade unions have nothing like the power they had in the post-war years and well into the 1970s, although the Butler and Tanner dispute of 2008 shows how important they can be still in protecting the interests of working people.

Anne Mitchard, a Frome girl who moved away from the town when she grew up, remembers both her mother and her father, as Frome people, being very much involved in local issues, as were many of the contributors in this book. Whilst her father, John Mitchard, had stood for parliament in the North Somerset constituency, her mother, Doreen, became a committed and proud JP, one of the first few women to be appointed.

Anne reflects on the town in which she grew up.

When we were growing up, we all thought of Frome as small and decidedly behind the times. In the Sixties and Seventies, when the media were beginning to sell us such an amazing new colourful world of clean lines and synthetic materials, parts of Frome like the Trinity area were slum-like. Much of the stone that is now a warm honey colour was black and grim. But it was home, and where we spent our happy childhoods: the cattle market, Paniccia's ice-cream, playing round the park, pictures on Saturday mornings at the Gaumont, discos up the Hexagon suite when we were older, and getting away with under-age drinking in the town centre pubs. **Anne Mitchard**

There we have it, then. Frome is now no longer the self-contained world it was once. It has grown and changed, just as the people whose memories are recorded in this book have grown and changed.

What we have recorded is that it was different in so many ways. The Frome where large-scale enterprise such as Singer's, the cattle market, Beswick's and Nott's Industries were located right in the heart of the town has become the Frome of smaller-scale employers, self-employed workers and commuters.

The town where everyone knew everyone else (and their business) has been replaced by a more private life-style. The world of television, the Internet and social media can seem much more real than everyday life in a small town in Somerset. The impersonal relationship with the supermarket has replaced many, though happily not all, of the face-to-face encounters across a shop counter, when news and gossip are exchanged as well as money and goods. Although many of the work clubs have disappeared along with the industries, sports clubs, societies and community groups continue to thrive in Frome.

Frome is an unusual and very special town. It is particularly fortunate in having kept a great many of the buildings and streets that link the present with the past and in having so many residents that can trace their histories back through generations and who care so deeply about the town. It is also fortunate in having been able to attract many newcomers with a wealth of ideas and a commitment to keeping alive the town's tradition of fiercely-guarded independence. Carnival, festivals, markets and independent shops continue to give pleasure to residents and visitors alike.

But it is Frome's long-established residents who have witnessed the transformations to their town and in their working lives, described in this book. Successful adaptation to these changes has required enormous resilience on their part. Despite everything, Frome is warm and welcoming with a strong sense of place and of belonging. In a word, home.

Index

This index includes the names of the contributors and firms mentioned in the book. References in **bold type** are to illustrations.